CW00827929

Using Illustrations in Expository Preaching

STORIES
THAT
SERVE

ED MOLL

I'm always impressed by how frequently and fluently many Ugandan preachers pepper their speech and sermons with local proverbs and parables, and how well-received and appreciated they often are by congregations. But integrating such "little stories" into a sermon in order to serve and teach listeners without being distracting or confusing can be tricky. I'm so grateful for Ed's help to do this effectively with this excellent little book, *Stories That Serve*. It's the most practical, applicable, clear and helpful guide to this topic I've yet found. I'm planning to apply these principles into my own preaching and will also be sharing this book widely with my students and colleagues to help them do the same.

Chris Howles
Head of Theology, Uganda Martyrs Seminary Namugongo, Kampala, Uganda
Founder, From Every Nation, https://www.fromeverynation.net/

Some of us leave church on Sunday talking about the amusing little story that the preacher shared in the sermon. But we can't for the life of us remember what the Bible passage was about. Ed Moll's wonderfully helpful book will enable his fellow preachers not to fall into this trap. The great strength of this book is its focus on the power of God's word to change human lives. Ed helps us to think about how little stories, our illustrations and applications, bring clarity not confusion to the exposition of Scripture, so that God's word is clearly understood. I wish I'd been able to read this book when I began my own preaching ministry thirty years ago; and I'd love to be able to share it with fellow preachers I've served alongside in England, Kenya and Australia.

David Williams
Director of Training and Development,
Church Missionary Society Australia

No doubt illustrations play a vital role in making sermons relevant. But as Ed Moll says, "We want neither big stories that swallow up the sermon nor no-stories that stifle it, but little stories that serve the sermon and allow the text to do the work." (p. 5). What "little stories," are, where can one find them and how and where in the sermon these can be used most effectively are valuable insights this book offers. If one wants to know how to give supporting help or how stories can help with clarity, this book is a guide.

Alongla Aier
Langham Preaching Movement Coordinator, Nagaland, India

Several authors have noted that one of the weaknesses of expository preaching is the lack of good illustrations, or what Ed Moll calls "little stories." Many of us have heard expository sermons with no stories at all and we know how difficult it is to follow and put into practice this type of preaching. This challenging book is for all who love expository preaching but don't know how to use little stories in their sermon.

Igor Améstegui
Langham Preaching Director, Latin America

Ed Moll has made a decisive contribution to helping us to understand illustration clearly, substantively and passionately. It's not simply about telling stories, it's about telling the stories that fit, a gift of the Spirit.

Jorge Atiencia
Langham Preaching Movement Coordinator, Latin America

Stories That Serve is short, well structured and easy to read – accessible. It is approachable enough for preachers who want to improve their sermon illustration skills on their own and a superb guide for designing interactive lessons for teachers of preaching.

Jennifer Cuthbertson, DMin
Langham Preaching Coordinator for Facilitator Development

This book is a concise and practical guide on how to use little stories to motivate, illustrate and resonate themes and ideas from biblical passages. It provides a structure and overview of different types of stories that are best suited for different forms of sermons. This should be read actively as the author includes different exercises to learn and apply the lessons in each chapter into the reader's own sermons and past preaching. Serious students of the Bible and pastors will benefit greatly from this concise resource.

Varunaj Churnai, PhD
Old Testament Professor, Bangkok Institute of Theology and Bangkok Bible Seminary
Christian Education Pastor, Sapanluang Klongton Church, Bangkok, Thailand
Langham Preaching Movement Coordinator, Thailand

When learning a new skill, it is far better to go to someone who had to learn it the hard way than someone who is just instinctively good at it (but cannot explain how they did it). The person who has had to work things out step-by-step is better placed to share their thought processes. From the time when he first started to preach, Ed Moll realized that he was not one of life's instinctive storytellers or sermon illustrators. But that is precisely why I always sit up and notice when he does preach; because he has considered carefully how to communicate well, he always manages to explain even complex truths with clarity and simplicity. It is also why this book is so helpful. I have learned so much from his methodical approach to illustrating better.

Mark Meynell, DMin
Langham Preaching Director, Europe & Caribbean

As a preacher, one of my ongoing struggles is finding and sharing the appropriate illustrations for my messages. I see the same challenge in pastors and leaders involved in Langham Preaching projects in Latin America. With clear concepts, recommendations and practical examples, Ed Moll not only gives us "the fish" but also "the hook and line" to fish for illustrations that help our listeners to understand, be motivated by, and apply the truths of God's word, communicated through a biblical sermon.

Dionisio Orjuela
Pastor, Shalom Christian Community, Ibague, Colombia
Langham Preaching Movement Coordinator, Central America

In the delivery of sermons, the criteria of clarity, faithfulness and relevance should be observed. Storytelling is a great way of communicating. Its powerful use has been exemplified by our master-teacher, Jesus Christ. The use of stories not only helps with illumination of the text but also with retention of the message. Moll's book serves as a great tool for seasoned expositors, as well as those who are seeking to hone their craft of expository preaching. This book is descriptive, highlighting the different types of stories. It is also illustrative, showing how stories could be used. Further, it is persuasive in arguing why stories should be used in preaching. There is much benefit to be derived from reading (and re-reading) this book. I highly recommend it.

Desmond Rogers
Langham Preaching Movement Coordinator, Caribbean

Ed Moll has produced an indispensable must-read tool for all preachers serious about expository preaching. He explains and demonstrates how "Explanatory," "Motivational" and "Exemplary" stories should be used in the points and between the points in a sermon to allow the passage to speak under the topic as God's word. As he puts it, he has given us a hook and line to fish for life and not just one meal. Get the book, read and apply the teachings and see our congregations grow in the knowledge of God's word.

Frank Shayi
Former Principal and Lecturer, International College of Bible and Missions,
Roodepoort, South Africa
Langham Preaching Regional Coordinator Emeritus, Southern Africa

Stories are said to be windows that shed light to a truth. An obscure idea becomes clear when a story is used to illustrate the point it is making. Stories are especially important in our sermons. Ed Moll introduces us to the different kinds of stories that we can use in our expository preaching. From his many years of pastoral and preaching experience, Moll shows us the advantages of using the right stories at the right place and the pitfalls of using the wrong stories. To be good storytellers, we need to learn the skills of storytelling. This is an excellent resource that will help anyone involved in preaching God's word to tell stories that will help our hearers grasp the message of the sermon. Ed Moll has given us a treasure that needs to be in the hands of pastors, teachers and laypersons who have committed their lives to preaching the word.

Frew Tamrat, PhD
Principal, Evangelical Theological College, Addis Ababa, Ethiopia
Langham Preaching Movement Coordinator, Ethiopia

Stories That Serve

Langham
PREACHING RESOURCES

Stories That Serve

Using Illustrations in Expository Preaching

Ed Moll

Langham

PREACHING RESOURCES

© 2022 Ed Moll

Published 2022 by Langham Preaching Resources
An imprint of Langham Publishing
www.langhampublishing.org

Langham Publishing and its imprints are a ministry of Langham Partnership

Langham Partnership
PO Box 296, Carlisle, Cumbria, CA3 9WZ, UK
www.langham.org

ISBNs:
978-1-83973-654-4 Print
978-1-83973-701-5 ePub
978-1-83973-702-2 Mobi
978-1-83973-703-9 PDF

British Library Cataloguing-in-Publication Data
A catalogue record for this book is available from the British Library

ISBN: 978-1-83973-654-4

Cover & Book Design: projectluz.com

Contents

Foreword

Ed Moll's *Stories That Serve* is not only a compelling guide to understand the affinity between our own stories and God's big story but also a great help on how to avoid common mistakes in relating or applying our own stories to sermons as we preach God's word.

Long before there was literacy or any form of writing, most parts of the world were used to storytelling. This is particularly true for the African context. We love oral stories and storytelling was the primary means of passing on information or knowledge about various life issues from generation to generation, be they in form of fable, folktale, myth or legend. Our identity, culture and response to issues of daily life are shaped by accounts of what happened in the past, which also have implications for the present and future. Accounts of heroes, events, history of clans and of nations as well as entertaining stories from the world of animals are often compelling

The beauty of *Stories That Serve* is the skilful reminder of the relationship between our own stories and the bigger story of God as recorded in the Holy Scriptures. Scripture as God's big story addresses all aspects of life and it is important to pay close attention, not only to how we read and interpret it, but also how we connect our own stories to it.

Moll affirms that there is a place for storytelling in preaching, provided that stories are rightly used. After all, the Lord Jesus Christ was the master storyteller, often teaching people through parables that relate to everyday life. Our challenge is often how to relate or apply the stories we love to God's big story in expository preaching. Our love of stories, as good as they are, need some boundaries when it comes to preparation of sermons and biblical preaching. Many of us must have experienced situations in which a preacher's story is so compelling that it overshadows the content and meaning of the biblical text being preached on. Rather than what the text is about, listeners often leave the service knowing more about the preacher's "big story" than the message and the meaning of the biblical text.

In the light of this Ed Moll warns us against using our own stories to overshadow God's word as revealed to us in the Holy Scriptures. However interesting or important our stories are, they must not become so big as to overshadow the biblical text or to impose various meanings contrary to that originally intended. Stories used in preaching must not become "big stories that swallow up the sermon" but remain "little stories that serve the sermon and allow the text to do the work." Moll also cautions us against using no stories at all in sermons, which may stifle preaching.

The use of stories in sermons, as good as they are, should also not mean doing away with structures. The discipline of adequate preparation with clear structures and well laid out points for sermons remains important. Moll's emphasis that stories used to illustrate any aspect need to fit into the structure of the sermon, should not be taken lightly.

Stories That Serve is so well written and illustrated. I wholeheartedly commend it to all preachers as a helpful tool on the use of stories as a bridge of connection between our day-to-day lived realities and the world of biblical texts; connection between preacher and listeners, as well as more, opens doors to clarity in biblical preaching.

Femi B. Adeleye
Director, Langham Preaching, Africa
Peduase, Ghana

Glossary of Terms

Expository preaching aims to explain and apply a single passage, with the theme determined by the text. Sometimes also called expositional preaching.

Thematic preaching takes a theme and develops it with reference to one or more biblical passages. The theme is taken to the passage rather than from the passage.

A *theme sentence* summarizes what the passage is about.

An *aim sentence* summarizes what the sermon invites people to do.

Big stories are longer stories which teach a moral or value through their plot and development and by their own authority.

Little stories are any of the following which support the teaching of the Bible:

- *Image:* a simple word picture.
- *Simple parable:* a word picture with a small amount of action.
- *Narrative:* a longer story with a beginning, a middle and an ending. Fables and longer parables are counted as narratives here.
- *Metaphor:* a mind picture that can draw together several ideas. Image rather than plot is central in a metaphor.
- *Explanatory story:* a little story that helps with understanding.
- *Motivational story:* a little story that moves us to action.
- *Exemplary story:* an example where the truth has been put into practice.

To *illustrate* means to use a little story for any of the above purposes. We have tried to avoid the noun "illustration" as it can mean either "little story" or "explanatory story."

Introduction

Big Stories and Little Stories

The north wind and the sun argued which was the stronger. On seeing a traveller they agreed a suitable test would be to strip him of his cloak. First the wind blew with all its might, but the more it blew, the more tightly the man wrapped the cloak around himself. When the sun's turn came, it gently beamed at the man, who loosened his cloak. The sun shone brighter still, and the man threw off his cloak.

That story is a fable ascribed to the ancient Greek storyteller Aesop and teaches that persuasion is more powerful than force. This tale is a starting place for our discussion about using stories in expository preaching, a practice that will greatly help our clarity, faithfulness and relevance.

Because we each have our own understanding of what preaching is and what stories are, the first task is to agree on the terms. Sometimes the same words can mean very different things to different people. For example to someone from the USA, "first floor" refers to ground level, but in British English the "first floor" is the storey above the ground floor. Imagine agreeing to meet on the first floor without agreeing terms! In the same way we need to agree what we mean by preaching and exposition.

Expository Preaching

Expository preaching is a form of preaching that aims to explain and then apply the message of a single Bible passage. The theme and topic for the sermon come from the text which is being expounded. The verb related to "expository" is "expounded," rather than the more logical "exposited." English is not a logical language! But it is also not a static language and, given time, it is likely that one day we will be able to say "exposited" and be correct! Expository preaching is also sometimes called expositional preaching. Whatever we call it, the goal is to teach and apply the main theme of a passage.

In contrast to expository preaching which draws the theme from the text, other forms of preaching bring the theme to the text. These include evangelistic preaching, whose aim is to bring truth to unbelievers; doctrinal or catechetical preaching, to teach truth to believers; festal preaching, to celebrate events in the church year such as Christmas, Easter and Pentecost; and prophetic preaching, to speak to a particular historical or cultural moment.[1] In these forms of thematic preaching, the theme is decided before the passage is chosen – assuming that there is even a connection between the two! The conviction behind expository preaching, however, is that because God speaks in and through his word, we listen to him best when we let the word do the talking. Faithful preaching therefore aims to open up a passage so that it sets the theme and topic. For more on the convictions behind expository preaching, please see the appendix.

Expository preaching changes both what we preach and how we preach. First, it changes what we preach, because we no longer bring the message to the text; instead we allow the text to bring God's word to us through the tools of exploration, interpretation and application. And when we preach our way sequentially through books of the Bible rather than picking a different passage each week, the church is further enriched because we learn to hear God's word in context. What we preach changes because we more clearly preach God's words than our own.

Expository preaching also changes how we preach, and this is seen most clearly in the part that stories play in our preaching. If you are new to expository preaching, you may have opportunity to hear others demonstrate it. At first your main response may be that this is very different preaching – foreign even. My hope is that this book will help you to see how stories feature in expository preaching, so that you can adopt and adapt this way of preaching in your own ministry. This will allow you to use what we are calling little stories in your preaching, and to do so with confidence.

If you are new to expository preaching, you may also be used to preaching either with what we are calling big stories or with no stories at all, instead of using what we are going to call little stories.

---

1. See Timothy Keller, *Preaching: Communicating Faith in an Age of Scepticism* (London: Hodder & Stoughton, 2015), 30. Although Conrad Mbewe divides preaching into evangelistic preaching that brings people into the people of God, and pastoral preaching that builds up the people of God, his focus in both is on what we here call expository preaching. Conrad Mbewe, *Pastoral Preaching: Building a People for God* (Carlisle: Langham Preaching Resources, 2017), 9–15.

Big Stories

Stories come in different shapes and sizes, which we will explore below. At heart a story is a narrative with characters and a plot. When the wind and the sun agree to a test, we are interested to see who will win and how. The plot is resolved when the sun wins. This story has a message that we can understand easily: persuasion is more powerful than force. Many of our cultures are filled with stories of this kind, which teach through the story. These are what we will call big stories, because the moral teaching is being done by the story and its plot. Big stories can be very powerful in shaping cultures, which is why they are handed down from generation to generation. For example, Conrad Mbewe writes:

> Africans love stories. A day in an African village ends with stories, when the evening meal is over and the children gather around the fire to listen to the family storyteller. As the sparks from the flames rise into the evening sky, the imagination of the hearers is captured by the skilful narration of folktales.

He goes on to describe how his relative's stories taught him wisdom:

> His stories were closer to life as we knew it, and the lessons learned were at our level. His stories taught us to obey our parents and respect the elderly. We also learnt the principles of sowing and reaping from this man's annual visits.[2]

If you grew up in a culture with big stories and you want to preach, it is tempting and natural to want to bring big stories into your preaching because they are so persuasive. After all, your goal is to persuade people, isn't it? In the Acts of the Apostles we see Paul speaking to persuade.[3] Paul himself explains that his ministry is to persuade people: "Since, then, we know what it is to fear the Lord, we try to persuade others. What we are is plain to God, and I hope it is also plain to your conscience" (2 Cor 5:11). But the problem with big stories is that they do the work that is rightly God's work. The power of Paul's persuasion was not in his words or his story, but in God's words and God's story: "Rather, we have renounced secret and shameful ways; we do not use deception, nor do we distort the word of God. On the contrary, by setting forth the truth plainly we commend ourselves to everyone's conscience in the sight of God" (2 Cor 4:2–3a). When big stories replace the persuasive power of

---

2. Mbewe, *Pastoral Preaching*, 125.

3. See, for example, Acts 17:4; 18:4, 13; 26:28; 28:23. Note that others can persuade too; for example, Acts 5:40 (Gamaliel); 6:11 (Stephen's opponents); 16:15 (Lydia).

God's word they become "secret and shameful ways" because the message being communicated does not come from God but from the culture. Aesop's fable of the wind and the sun is not rooted in Scripture but in common wisdom. The task of expository preaching is to take the truth we have received in Scripture and to set it forth plainly.

There are maybe two ways in which big stories can be used in faithful preaching. I will mention them here but they are not the subject of this book. The first is in first-person preaching in which the speaker tells a story as if they were a character within the story. For example we could hear the imagined thoughts of Mary as she experienced the emotional roller-coaster of the week between Jesus's triumphal entry to Jerusalem and his burial on Good Friday; or the tension and fear of an Israelite first-born child on the night of the Passover, waiting to see whether the blood of the lamb will be effective to save. Provided that the focus is clearly on Christ, and that the details fit with what is provided in Scripture, this may be an effective way to communicate. The second way is where a big story from outside the Bible has a message that is clearly and explicitly aligned with the message of a biblical sermon. In both of these cases, the story is bigger than the sermon. We could say that the story has swallowed the sermon as surely as the whale (or fish) swallowed Jonah! Our concern here is with using little stories in preaching.

No Stories

The opposite error of allowing big stories to swallow the sermon is to preach with no stories at all. To some this will seem very strange indeed. They have been taught never to make a point without a story. And never to tell a story without a point. We have to recognize that in some educational systems, thinkers are taught to develop their points by logical and linear arguments, one point after another. I have to say that while this is very helpful for organizing thoughts and arguments, it makes for very dull sermons. I have heard many thematic sermons developed in this way: the speaker first announces the theme or the thesis to be developed, and then supports the thesis with detailed logical arguments.

Others among us may be concerned that preaching through stories undermines our commitment to truth. Christians are convinced that we can make true statements about who God is and what he has done: these are sometimes called propositional truths. Because there are truths about God that we need to know in order to know God, we need to preach in a way that declares these truths. For example, when Peter speaks to Cornelius and his household, he begins by declaring what they know about God (propositional truths):

> You *know* the message God sent to the people of Israel, announcing the good news of peace through Jesus Christ, who is Lord of all. You *know* what has happened throughout the province of Judea, beginning in Galilee after the baptism that John preached – how God anointed Jesus of Nazareth with the Holy Spirit and power, and how he went around doing good and healing all who were under the power of the devil, because God was with him.
>
> We are witnesses of everything he did in the country of the Jews and in Jerusalem. They killed him by hanging him on a cross. (Acts 10:36–39, emphasis added)

The desire to preach God's truth in a rational, logical, careful fashion wants to honour the task of building God's people. We must acknowledge the good intention here while stating that we cannot expect such preaching to bring about a response, humanly speaking. If the truth is presented without light, it is dull; and if it is dull, how can it lead to obedience? Our desire is for understanding that leads to obedience. The solution is not to avoid stories altogether but to use them well. For that reason, preachers brought up within this tradition started to add little stories and word pictures, to bring a little light into the pulpit. For congregations brought up with dull philosophical treatises, even this was a breath of fresh air.

I think this background of preaching with no stories explains why two great twentieth-century British preachers seemed to use so few stories. They were starting from a culture that assumed no stories. The preaching of Dr. Martyn Lloyd-Jones was described as "logic on fire," which surely reveals the culture's appreciation of head over heart. His contemporary John Stott was also sparing in the use of little stories, although he encouraged others to use them. In fact Stott and Lloyd-Jones did use images and stories but so skilfully that their brushwork cannot be seen: Stott was the master of the one-line parable, while Lloyd-Jones used many vivid images. These men were masters of the little story in preaching, and a rebuke to those who thought it God-honouring to use no stories at all.

Little Stories

So we want neither big stories that swallow up the sermon, nor no-stories that stifle it, but little stories that serve the sermon and allow the text to do the work.

Naturally we are afraid that once we let stories into our sermon they will take over like a weed. I remember one well-known preacher who spoke without a break and without notes for nearly an hour, which was a long time by the standards of that church. The staff reflected on the sermon during the following week. It was when they tried to sum up the message that they realized how light the sermon was on biblical content. The text could have been explained in ten minutes; the rest was just stories. He had used too many stories – far more than were needed. We do not need to shy away from stories but ask instead what the right use of stories looks like. After all, Jesus himself used images and stories in his preaching. How often does he say "The kingdom of heaven is like . . ."? If we need further persuasion, let us remember that the Bible is full of stories and images. God uses stories, images, metaphors and all kinds of styles of writing to speak truth to us. How can we use little stories in our preaching?

Jesus was the master storyteller but, as Bryan Chapell points out, even his stories need explanation. Someone has calculated that about three quarters of Jesus's recorded teaching is image and story. We should not be surprised that the creator of the whole-of-life calls us to follow him in the whole-of-life using images and stories drawn from the whole-of-life.[4] We will see that our preaching too can use little stories drawn from the whole of life.

Stories also engage the whole person. American church planter and preacher Timothy Keller explains: "The essence of a good illustration . . . is to evoke a remembered sense experience and bring it into connection with a principle. That makes the truth real both by helping listeners better understand it and by inclining their hearts more to love it."[5] In other words, we are more likely to understand and believe what we can feel. In a greater way, we may know in our heads that depression is a dark experience, but we come closer to appreciating the truth when we hear or read a vivid first-hand description of how it feels for a sufferer to wake each morning to find that once again the joy has leaked out of his or her world.

Third, we will see that using little stories in our preaching will help our clarity, because using them makes us think more carefully about our sermon, how it is constructed and how it works. I believe that using little stories in preaching is all part of what Paul asks for in Colossians 4:4: "Pray that I may proclaim it [our message] clearly, as I should."

---

4. Bryan Chapell, *Christ-Centered Preaching: Redeeming the Expository Sermon*, 2nd rev. ed. (Grand Rapids, MI: Baker Academic, 2005), 185, 187 n. 42, 189.

5. Keller, *Preaching*, 173.

How then do we do it? I suggest three steps. First, we will briefly outline the different kinds of stories that we can understand as "little stories." Second, we will consider how little stories can fit within the points of a sermon; and third, we will look at stories that fit between the points of a sermon. These assume a basic sermon outline which we will also mention.

You will find that we seem to speed up because the chapters in the second part are shorter than in the first part. This represents the gradual handing over of responsibility from my setting out the foundations to you taking the ideas and putting them to work in your setting.

Exercises are found throughout the text and these can be done on your own or with others. Many have found it helpful to belong to a preaching club to discover expository preaching together, and these exercises would be good food for discussion together.

For Further Reading

Chapell, Bryan. *Christ-Centered Preaching: Redeeming the Expository Sermon*. 2nd rev. ed. Grand Rapids, MI: Baker Academic, 2005.

Keller, Timothy. *Preaching: Communicating Faith in an Age of Scepticism*. London: Hodder & Stoughton, 2015.

Mbewe, Conrad. *Pastoral Preaching: Building a People for God*. Carlisle: Langham Preaching Resources, 2017.

1

Different Kinds of Stories and How They Fit within a Sermon

So far we have distinguished between what we call big stories and little stories. Big stories are like the fables and tales that we inherit through our culture, longer and emotionally compelling stories that deliver a powerful moral. First-person sermons, in which the whole sermon is a story, might also come under this category. The point about big stories is that they do the work. If we imagine digging a hole, we would say that big stories wield the spade while the Bible text stands by and watches. In expository preaching, however, we want the places to be switched: because God's word is powerful, we want to allow it to do the work (or more correctly, to allow God's Holy Spirit to do the work), and then add our little stories to give supporting help. Little stories fit within a sermon, whereas big stories will swallow the sermon up.

Different Kinds of Little Stories

"Little stories" is a term to cover several different kinds of pictures that we paint using words, and in this section we will explore them and define the ways we will use the terms in this book. Each of these words can be used in different ways, and other writers and speakers will vary in their use of them, which is why it is necessary to define what we mean here. For instance, "illustration" is used by some writers for any story used to help expound a passage, but by others it refers only to stories that help with understanding. For that reason we will use "little story" instead. In the rest of this book, we use "little story" to refer to *any* of the following kinds.

An *image* or *word picture* is the simplest little story. Like a photograph, it gives an instant snapshot. James paints the picture of a patient farmer when he says, "See how the farmer waits for the land to yield its valuable crop, patiently waiting for the autumn and spring rains." Jesus tells the church at Laodicea that he is near when he says, "Here I am! I stand at the door and knock. If anyone hears my voice and opens the door, I will come in and eat with that person, and they with me." And Peter uses a word picture to encourage his readers to be self-controlled and alert because "your enemy the devil prowls around like a roaring lion looking for someone to devour."[1]

A *simple parable* takes a word picture and adds a small amount of action. If the image is like a still photograph, the short parable is like a very short video clip (or a GIF file) that can be circulated on social media. New wine into old wineskins and new cloth sewn onto old are both short parables, as is Jesus's saying that "if the blind lead the blind, both will fall into a pit."[2] A few words paint the whole picture.

A *narrative* is longer than a simple parable because it has a beginning, a middle and an ending. Many of the longer parables of Scripture are narratives – for example, Nathan's parable to expose King David's hypocrisy, adultery and murder, or Jesus's parable of the sower. Fables are also narratives, such as Jotham's fable in which the trees ask the thorn to rule over them, with disastrous consequences.[3]

Preaching the New Testament parables is a whole subject in itself: they are mentioned here only in order to illustrate that longer parables that have a beginning, a middle and an end are all types of narrative.[4]

The story is told of a Scottish pastor visiting a church member who had stopped attending church. At this man's home, a coal fire was burning in the grate. The minister took one of the glowing coals from the fire and put it away on the side of the hearth. Slowly the coal cooled and stopped glowing. Then the pastor replaced the coal among the others, and it started to glow again. The point of the story was to remind the old church member that his love for the Lord would grow cold if he too held himself at a distance from the Lord's people. This story is both a simple parable and a narrative: the pastor's action of lifting the coal was a simple parable; the story of the pastor's visit is a narrative.

A *metaphor* is a mind picture that can draw together several ideas. Metaphor, in the sense we are using it here, works across a number of levels.

---

1. Jas 5:7; Rev 3:20; 1 Pet 5:8.

2. Matt 9:16–17; 15:14.

3. 2 Sam 12; Matt 13:1–23 and parallel passages; Judg 9:8–15.

4. See, for example, Mark Meynell, *What Angels Long to Read: Reading and Preaching the New Testament* (Carlisle: Langham Preaching Resources, 2017), ch. 7, "Preaching Jesus's Stories."

Unlike an image, a metaphor works at more than one level and acquires a life of its own. Unlike a narrative where the plot is central, in a metaphor the image is central. Many of the images in the Psalms can work as metaphors. For example, Psalm 1 says that the person whose delight is in the law of the Lord is "like a tree planted by streams of water."[5] It becomes a metaphor in the hands of the preacher who uses the picture of the tree to connect several related ideas. Hear how US pastor Timothy Keller picks up this idea of the tree's stability as one of the benefits of meditation:

> The person experienced in meditation is like a tree rooted so that the wind cannot blow it away. Notice that this tree is planted by streams of water. Trees by streams do well even if there is little rain. This is an image of someone who can keep going in hard, dry times.[6]

The tree's stability contrasts with the chaff that is so easily blown away by the wind (Ps 1:4). The tree bears fruit only in season but has leaves all year round, so "meditation leads to stability – the tree is an evergreen! – but not to complete immunity from suffering and dryness." And then, third, Keller draws on the tree to illustrate the heart aspect of meditation: "Meditation is likened to tree roots taking in water. That means not merely knowing a truth but taking it inside and making it a part of yourself."[7] The tree has become a metaphor drawing together several strands of thought, each of which works at a different level. There is an important caution here: we must not allow metaphors to lead us beyond what Scripture says.

In a similar way, Zambian pastor Conrad Mbewe uses a farming metaphor to describe the role that pastoral preaching plays in shepherding the people of God:

> Many people enter pastoral ministry with only a vague idea about what work awaits them in pastoral preaching. Hence they end up like goats, wandering around nibbling on one blade of grass after another until they get lost because they do not know where they

---

5. Ps 1:3. This is strictly also a simile – the person is "like" a tree. Metaphors and similes are sometimes hard to tell apart.

6. Timothy Keller, *Prayer: Experiencing Awe and Intimacy with God* (London: Hodder & Stoughton, 2014), 146.

7. Keller, 147, 150.

ought to be going. And once the pastor is lost, the congregation
is also lost.[8]

It is a lovely metaphor that if the shepherds do not care for the flock of God,
they become goats that get lost!

These then are the different kinds of stories we will talk about in this
book: image or word picture; simple parable; narrative (which includes longer
parables); and metaphor.

Finally, when we use a little story – of any of the kinds described above – we
call it "illustrating." Although there is a slight risk of confusion with the noun
"illustration" (which we are trying to avoid using), there is no single word for
"using little stories to explain." So "to illustrate" is to use a little story for any
of the purposes we are describing.

How do little stories fit within a sermon?

How Stories Fit into Sermons

Preachers who find their own voice will deliver very different kinds of sermons.
We can think of them as different types of tapestries. Some of us use precise
language and linear logic, like creating a geometric design. Others paint a scene
with authentic figures and bright colours: African scenes if we are African,
cityscapes if we are urban, and so on. Some use colour sparingly, others splash
it around. We will preach in as many different ways as weavers weave. However,
if we turn any tapestry over, we will see that despite their differences they have
a common underlying structure: the framework of cords that run from top to
bottom and which support the coloured threads. The parts of a tapestry may
have different names in each language but the hidden structure will be the
same whatever the outward design. I would suggest that the basic structure that
underlies a simple sermon is like those cords that support the coloured threads.
These elements are present, in one way or another, in any basic expository
sermon. The aim of expository preaching is to make the main point that the
Bible passage is making. When we have outlined the basic sermon structure
we will be able to see where little stories fit either within the points or between
the points. This allows us to fit the right story at the right point.

---

8. Mbewe, *Pastoral Preaching*, 2.

A Basic Sermon Structure

The apostle Paul was not too proud to use simple but effective ways of speaking because he said, "When I came to you, I did not come with eloquence or human wisdom as I proclaimed to you the testimony about God. For I resolved to know nothing while I was with you except Jesus Christ and him crucified" (1 Cor 2:1–2). Just as a musician learns the basic chords to build a foundation for writing his or her own songs later on, so we can learn from this basic method. At its simplest, the following is the basic structure for a simple sermon.

The basic sermon has an introduction, a number of points, and a conclusion. Each point aims to explain and apply a section or aspect of the Bible passage so that between them the points communicate the whole point of the whole passage. The conclusion draws together the threads without introducing new material. Dividing the sermon into points really helps with clarity because it means we are speaking about one idea at a time. Our different cultural styles should not change the fact that our sermon needs to begin well, is helped by developing the ideas one at a time, and needs to finish well.[9] Usually between two and four points is enough:

- Introduction
- First point
- Second point
- Third point
- Conclusion

The basic outline for developing a point also contains certain elements. They are set out below in a linear way, but it may be that different styles and cultures will develop points in a slightly different way. Nevertheless, all the elements need to be present. It is like a meal in which there are meat, rice, vegetables and fruit. In some places fruit is eaten first, in others it acts as a dessert. Whatever the order, all the elements are needed for a full meal, and in the same way all the elements below are needed to make a point.

We begin by stating the point. Whether we announce it, number it and write it on a board, or whether we simply start on it is less important than being clear in our minds what it is we are going to spend the next few minutes developing. The second element is to support the point and explain it, sometimes also called "explain and validate." Explanation will involve clarifying words used in the passage, such as "Pharisee" or "justification" or "sin," or

---

9. For example, Conrad Mbewe, writing in Africa for African preachers, uses a very similar outline. Mbewe, 107–8.

place names and so on. Validation means showing where in the passage the idea came from. I invariably point to the verse and then read it out. Next we illustrate with a little story that comes alongside the explanation to help it along. Notice that God's word is doing the work because we have started with the biblical text and its explanation. The text is holding the spade and doing the digging: the little story is holding the bucket. After the little story (illustration) we restate the point, if possible drawing together words used in the little story and the explanation to show the connection. Then we apply the point, showing what this truth means for us today. In some cases this isn't possible until we have made several points, and the application comes later in the whole sermon. While each of us may develop points in a different way, it does not seem to me possible to develop a point without stating it; nor to develop a point from the Bible without explanation and validation; nor to preach without inviting a response, that is, application. The transformative strength of expository preaching is that when all these elements line up, we allow God to speak clearly and powerfully because the application flows from the main point, and the main point flows from the passage.

1. State the point.

2. Support the point and explain it.

3. Illustrate (little story).

4. Restate.

5. Apply the point.

This is a reliable way to be clear and relevant, even though it is simple.

Stories can either work *within* the points of the sermon, or *between* the points of the sermon.

Stories That Fit within the Main Points

Little stories that belong within the main points may broadly be called "sermon illustrations." But that can still be confusing because of the different ways these work. Here are three ways we might use little stories within a point.

Explanatory stories are images, short parables or narratives that help with understanding. They link abstract ideas, which we cannot experience, with objects or situations, which we can experience. This kind of little story is mainly used for illumination and acts like a window that lets light into a room. John Stott explains: "In order to see we need light, and the word 'illustrate' means to illumine, to throw light or lustre upon an otherwise dark object. It is for this reason that illustrations have sometimes been likened to the windows of a house." Similarly, Conrad Mbewe says that these kinds of stories make the eyes of the mind "see" the point that is being made in the sermon.[10] For example, we could tell the following story to illustrate how the seeming defeat of the cross hid the final victory of the resurrection: Imagine that the national football teams of Egypt and Ghana are playing in the final of the Africa Cup of Nations. You are with your Ghanaian friend, but in a place with a poor mobile signal. You await a text that will give the result. Eventually it comes: "Ghana defeated . . . [message interrupted]." The mobile signal has been lost and your friend is inconsolable. Ghana have once again lost to their long-term rivals. Then the phone beeps again. The signal has been restored and the full message has come through. It reads, "Ghana defeated Egypt." Your mourning turns to rejoicing. And so it was in a very much bigger way for the disciples when they realized that "Jesus defeated" at the cross hid the greater truth that "Jesus defeated death" by his resurrection.[11] The little story of the lost signal has helped us to understand. It is an *explanatory story*.

Motivational stories engage our emotions as well as our minds and move us to action. They are usually narratives rather than images or short parables. They warm the heart as the sun shining through the windows can warm a room. Good narratives make us care about the characters in the story, whether fictional or real. It seems that God gave us stories because he wanted us to experience salvation as well as understand it. Bryan Chapell goes even further by saying that "*the primary purpose of illustration is not to clarify but to motivate.*" Often we know what we need to do: but we need help to get out of our chairs and do it, as Chapell's fellow American Tim Keller explains: "Whatever captures the heart's trust and love also controls the feelings and behavior. What the heart most wants the mind finds reasonable, the emotions find valuable, and the will finds doable."[12] I have found that for American writers on preaching, "illustrations" tend to be motivational stories, while for British writers "illustrations" tend to be explanatory stories. Both are valid, but this is helpful to bear in mind if you are reading Western preaching literature. That is also why we use the terms little story, explanatory story, motivational story and exemplary story in preference to calling them illustrations.

---

10. John R. W. Stott, *I Believe in Preaching* (London: Hodder & Stoughton, 1982), 239–40; Mbewe, 108.

11. UK readers may recognize this as a version of the Waterloo story told by Mark Meynell, *Cross-Examined* (Nottingham: IVP, 2010), 121; Vaughan Roberts, *Turning Points* (Milton Keynes: Authentic, 1999), 135.

12. Chapell, *Christ-Centered Preaching*, 186, emphasis original; Keller, *Preaching*, 159.

This distinction is not new. Augustine of Hippo wrote *On Christian Teaching* in the fourth century AD to explain how Christians should understand and teach the Bible. He states that, in common with other forms of speaking, the purpose of preaching is to inform, delight and move our hearers, where "delight" means to make our hearers care about the truths we are setting forth. Explanatory stories help us to inform while motivational stories help us to move and delight.[13]

Exemplary stories are situations that show us where the truth has been put into practice. They put flesh onto the bones of the application. They are like looking out of the window so that we can see what our idea looks like in normal daily life – which is what happens outside the sermon. Exemplary stories show us how to live out the implications of this Bible passage in our own lives. For example, I vividly remember the story someone shared with me about how he put into daily practice the command to "pray continually" (1 Thess 5:17). This older Christian told me that he put this verse into practice by praying quickly and quietly before answering the telephone and also every time he walked past a particular door in the office building. His story was not strictly for illumination because the two words in that short verse are clear; neither did he motivate me to pray; rather his story gave me a practical example that showed me the way. It was especially helpful because I was working in an office at the time.

These three story types belong *within* a point because their role is to make the point clear, relevant and real to the hearer. We can add them to our list:

- State the point.
- Support the point and explain it.
- Illustrate (little story). (Explanatory story fits here. Motivational story also possible.)
- Restate.
- Apply the point (motivational story or exemplary story).

Stories That Belong between the Main Points

As well as using little stories within each main point to develop the point, we can place them between or around the main points to improve the sermon

---

13. Saint Augustine, *On Christian Teaching*, trans. R. P. H. Green (Oxford: Oxford University Press, 2008), 117.

as a whole. Here are some common uses of little stories used between the main points.

The *introduction*, as is commonly said, is the last part to be written and the first to be spoken. The aim of the introduction is to raise the topic and to gain the hearers' attention. There are many different ways to achieve this: we can ask questions, we can introduce a problem, or we can simply state our theme. We can also tell a story which ends up asking the very question that the passage addresses. For example, we could begin with the fable of the wind and the sun to introduce the question of how preachers are called to persuade others.

We may also need to use the introduction to gain our hearers' trust, especially if we are a visiting speaker or we are speaking to unbelievers who need to be convinced that we are worth listening to! Professional public speakers often begin with a number of light-hearted stories before their talk proper gets under way. We have better tools at our disposal, and they include telling a story that captures the audience's interest and convinces them that you're worth listening to.

Depending on the length of the sermon, the stamina of the congregation and our ability as speakers, we may also need stories to help the congregation avoid exhaustion or boredom. We do not have to do this, and often the stories within our main points will give enough breathing space. But there are times when listeners simply need to catch their breath before the next point. I remember a university lecturer who was popular although his subject was very difficult. Exactly halfway through a lecture he would stop lecturing and tell a funny short story. He was not a naturally humorous person and he did not tell the stories so much as read them from index cards. But we appreciated the breathing space he gave us to help us concentrate on his complex subject. If the sermon is on a difficult topic, we may need to help our hearers' concentration. The purpose of this kind of story is to allow hearers to regroup and recharge before continuing to the main point. It is a bonus if that story links to the main theme.

A third type of little story that belongs around the points is one that acts as a *conclusion* to the whole sermon. We should never introduce new material in the conclusion, and for that reason we should not be using the kinds of little stories that belong within a main point. Yet we can make a powerful ending to a sermon with something that brings the hearer back to the point of decision. It will look very much like a motivational story. For example, the following story has been used many times and in many different forms in connection with the parable of the prodigal son (Luke 15:11–24): There was a girl by the name of Christina who lived in a certain country. She wanted to see the bright lights of the city, as many teenagers do – and so she used to talk about it, and fantasize about it, and torture her mother about it. One day Maria, her mother, went into Christina's bedroom in the morning to waken her for school, only to find that she was gone – her clothes taken with her. So this is what Maria did: she went and packed a bag, went down to the bus station and got a ticket to the big city, where she believed Christina had gone. Before getting on the bus she went to a photo kiosk at the bus station and took as many photos of herself as she could afford, one after the other, and put them in a bag. She then got the bus, got to the city, and spent as many days as she could afford putting all the photographs up all over the place – in phone booths, in foyers of restaurants and hotels, on toilet mirrors – in the hope that Christina, somewhere, somehow, would see one. Eventually, just as happened to the prodigal son, Christina's money ran out and she took shameful work to earn a little more. One day, as she was walking through a hotel, she saw in the corner of the mirror in the foyer a picture of her mother. Her eyes began to fill with tears as she walked up to it, plucked it down, turned it over, and read these words on the back: "Christina, whatever you've done, whatever you've been, whatever you've become, come home. Come home."

Finally, a single story can link all the parts of the sermon. This can be a metaphor, such as the images of the tree or the goats (see above under "Different Kinds of Little Stories"). This running theme holds the whole sermon together and links the points. A visual aid or object can also be used in the same way.[14] We need to be careful that this little story does not overwhelm the sermon and become a big story that swallows the sermon. We also need to ensure that we do not develop the metaphor further than the Bible does. That is why the step of validating our points from the text is essential.

We must remember that when we divide stories into explanatory stories, motivational stories and exemplary stories, we are teasing apart threads that often belong together. This will feel artificial because stories can do more than one thing at a time, but in order to understand how they serve the sermon, we need to ask about the *most important* role that the story is playing here. Then we can tailor the story to our needs and weave it seamlessly into the sermon for best effect.

- Introduction (little story to raise a theme)
- First point
- Second point

---

14. See Help #48 in Langham Partnership, *Helps: 20 Simple and Memorable Teaching and Preaching Resources*, vol. 2 (Carlisle: Langham Preaching Resources, 2019), 14.

(Breather story if needed)

- Third point
- Conclusion (motivational story to draw together the threads)

Or, using a running metaphor:

- Introduction (introduce the metaphor and link to first point)
- First point
  (Return to metaphor and link to second point)
- Second point
  (Return to metaphor and link to third point)
- Third point
- Conclusion (wrap up metaphor and draw together the threads)

How we tell the story can connect us with our hearers. We can show we understand their world by telling stories that take place within it; or we can gain their trust because we show that we know what it is like to wrestle with the difficult questions they face. That is why we need to know how to use the right story in the right place.

Exercise

Look back at the last two or three sermons that you preached. Identify the stories, images and parables that you used. Which acted as stories that belong *within* the main points, and which were *between* the main points? What was their purpose, using our divisions of explanatory story, motivational story, exemplary story, introduction, breather story or conclusion?

For Further Reading

Langham Partnership. *Helps: 40 Simple and Memorable Teaching and Preaching Resources*. Volume 1. Carlisle: Langham Preaching Resources, 2019. Available from Langham Preaching: https://langhamliterature.org/preachinghelps.

Langham Partnership. "*Helps: 20 Simple and Memorable Teaching and Preaching Resources.*" Volume 2. Carlisle: Langham Preaching Resources, 2019. Available from Langham Preaching: https://langhamliterature.org/preachinghelps..

Meynell, Mark. *What Angels Long to Read: Reading and Preaching the New Testament.* Carlisle: Langham Preaching Resources, 2017. Especially chapter 7, "Preaching Jesus's Stories."

Stott, John R. W. *I Believe in Preaching*. London: Hodder & Stoughton, 1982.

2

Using Explanatory Stories for Illumination

Explanatory Stories Need a Point to Explain

I remember working with a dear man who laboured alongside me in preaching. He was and is a delightful Christian but his sermons were very difficult to follow. After listening to my preaching for a while he realized that he needed to start using little stories in his sermons, and specifically explanatory stories. That was when I understood why following his talks was so difficult. Not only did he not use little stories in his preaching, but he did not even divide his sermons into points. He was just rambling in the pulpit. Before he could think about introducing little stories, he first needed to learn to make points in his preaching. Explanatory stories can only work if they have a point to explain.

One way to think about making points in a sermon is to imagine that our task is to plant a flag on the summit of a hill. The hill represents the point being made, and the top of the hill is the central truth in the point being made. The

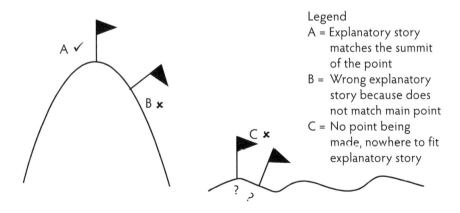

Legend
A = Explanatory story matches the summit of the point
B = Wrong explanatory story because does not match main point
C = No point being made, nowhere to fit explanatory story

flag represents the explanatory story. We are clearest when the explanatory story and the point being made are exactly aligned – that is, when the flag is planted dead centre on the top of the hill. If we plant our flag elsewhere, we will not be clear. This is why we first need to know what point is being made.

Let's try this with a worked example. Consider Matthew 24:36–44:

> But about that day or hour no one knows, not even the angels in heaven, nor the Son, but only the Father. As it was in the days of Noah, so it will be at the coming of the Son of Man. For in the days before the flood, people were eating and drinking, marrying and giving in marriage, up to the day Noah entered the ark; and they knew nothing about what would happen until the flood came and took them all away. That is how it will be at the coming of the Son of Man. Two men will be in the field; one will be taken and the other left. Two women will be grinding with a hand mill; one will be taken and the other left.
>
> Therefore keep watch, because you do not know on what day your Lord will come. But understand this: if the owner of the house had known at what time of night the thief was coming, he would have kept watch and would not have let his house be broken into. So you also must be ready, because the Son of Man will come at an hour when you do not expect him.

If I were preaching this passage, my first point might be that Jesus *will* return. What about the second point?

Exercise

(Try not to read ahead!) If the second point of a sermon on this passage is "Jesus's return will be . . . ," what is the missing word?

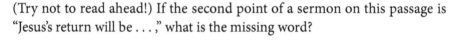

In the first draft of my sermon the second point was "Jesus's return will be *certain.*" I then looked for explanatory stories to help people to see this. Since there are three short parables in the passage (the people of Noah's day, the men in the field and the women at the mill), I looked to see how they illustrate my point that Jesus's return will be *certain.* And they don't! They are stories about something happening *suddenly*, as a complete surprise. This made me realize that the three stories in the passage did not fit the point I was making. I was trying to plant my flag on the side of the hill and not on the top. It is true that Jesus's return will be certain, but that is not the point being made *in this passage*. So I revised my second point to "Jesus's return will be *sudden*." Now the explanatory stories of the people in Noah's day, the two men in the field and the two women at the mill fit the point being made – that Jesus's return will be sudden. Every explanatory story needs a point to explain, and the better the story and the point are aligned, the clearer our preaching will be.

Finding the Best Fit between Explanatory Stories and the Point They Explain

The fit between the little story and the point being made is so important that we must press into it a bit further. Let us say that as well as using the three little stories in the passage we wanted to use an explanatory story from outside the passage. Can we find a story that will help link us to the application of verse 44: "So you also must be ready, because the Son of Man will come at an hour when you do not expect him"?

Exercise

Here are four possible explanatory stories that I found to go with this point:

(1) The weather in the hills and mountains can change very quickly. It can be warm and sunny when you set off on a walk, but within less than an hour you can find yourself in dangerous wind and rain. The warning for hillwalkers is to be prepared before you begin walking. It is not enough to think you are safe because you see no clouds when you set off.

(2) Yellowstone National Park in the USA sits on top of the world's largest active volcano, which could erupt at any moment. When author Bill Bryson asked about the evacuation plan in case of eruption he was told there isn't one: if the volcano blows, the eruption will be so sudden that no one will have time to escape.

(3) Agatha Christie's murder mystery *The Body in the Library* (1942) turns in part on the fragile health of rich Mr Jefferson. He has such a weak heart that a sudden shock might be fatal for him. Would the terrible news that someone he cares for has been murdered be enough to cause a heart attack? Probably not, because someone would take care to break the news carefully. A more likely danger is a door slamming in the wind, a sudden loud noise for which there has been no preparation or notice. The door would slam without warning, the shock would be sudden and Mr Jefferson might die.

(4) One of my all-time favourite stories is of Sir Ernest Shackleton and his expedition to the South Pole in 1914. It was a disaster followed by the most amazing rescue. The ship was caught in pack ice and crushed. The men escaped in lifeboats to a rock named Elephant Island. There were no radios, and no prospect of anyone passing by, so Shackleton and a handful of others sailed 800 miles (1300 km) to the island of South Georgia while Captain Frank Wild and the rest of the crew stayed on Elephant Island. Can you imagine what it must have been like for those men to see their only hope of rescue sail over the horizon, with no idea of when they might return – if ever? Once Shackleton reached South Georgia, it took him a further three months to charter a vessel for the rescue. Yet every day, Wild had his men roll up their sleeping bags, ready to jump on board the rescue vessel: "Roll up your bags, men, the boss may be coming today." And one day he did come, as they saw his boat come into sight. Shackleton's return was not soon. But it was certain. And they were ready.

What do you think of these explanatory stories? Which do you think works best and why?

_____

_____

_____

Analysis

A major concern is whether an Agatha Christie story set in wartime Britain will connect with anyone we are speaking to, in the UK or elsewhere. Our stories need to connect with the people we are speaking to. I remember when, on my first visit to Burkina Faso in West Africa, I told a little story about a ship and a lighthouse. I was halfway through the story when it dawned on me that there are no lighthouses in that land-locked country! My little story was going to make no sense to my hearers, let alone shed any light on the point I was trying to make from the passage. In the same way, the Agatha Christie story is outside most people's experience, and for that reason I would look for a different little story to use here.

The Agatha Christie story is also ineffective because the sudden noise of the door slamming is a concern only for poor Mr Jefferson's weak heart, whereas

Jesus's return will affect everyone, whether their hearts are healthy or not. The story does not fit well enough.

Antarctic expeditions are also beyond most people's experience, but a gripping story told well might work – just. But even if this story will work in your context, it does not belong to this part of the sermon because it illustrates the wrong point. The story tells us how Captain Wild ensured that, if and when Shackleton returned, his men would be ready for him. He was motivating his men rather than puzzling over whether he would see signs of the rescue mission. There was no prospect of advance notice in the South Atlantic in 1916: there were no radios, no passing ships. The first he would know of the rescue would be when he saw Shackleton's boat appear on the horizon. The real question is whether it would take place at all. Having said all that, this is a great motivational story to help us to be ready for Jesus's return.

The National Park story also has problems. The first is that we need to explain about volcanoes and craters in order to set the scene, and depending on our context that may or may not be a problem. The main difficulty about the story is that if the volcano erupts, no one will escape. The point of Jesus's story is to warn his hearers so that those who take steps to be ready for his return will escape.

That is why I think the hillwalking story works best, because those hikers who are always prepared will take adequate clothing and equipment and will be protected if the weather should change suddenly. One *can* take steps against changeable weather, but there is nothing you can do about an unpredictable volcano. This story is not without weakness, however. It works well in mountainous regions, but not, for example, in sub-Saharan Africa. I could possibly tell this as a story from my own experience: and it is a true story that I once trekked in some beautiful high mountains with a camp just below the summit. Since the weather was clear, a friend and I left our rucksacks for the short walk to the highest point of the trek. The weather changed very suddenly and we were caught out. I remember spending a long, very cold night in deep snow without either a sleeping bag or an extra coat. We were very fortunate not to have suffered worse. I now know that the weather in the mountains can change suddenly. I know that "suddenly" means there will be no warning and that I need to be ready at all times. Telling this story might be better than asking the people in a sandy country to imagine walking in the mountains – but the story needs to be told very well.

Please don't lose heart at this point! It does take work to find just the right little story to fit with a point, but when the two line up the effect is amazing, and the help we can give to others is truly worth it. We are allowing the light of

God's word to shine clearly into the hearts of our listeners, just as the gardener who trims a tree allows the light of the sun to bring life to his or her vegetable patch. As you read this you may already be thinking of little stories that are more closely adapted to your context and culture.

Connecting the Point and the Little Story by Restating Your Point

Once we have found our explanatory story and matched it to the point, it is time to link it back to the main point. At this stage we want to pick up words and phrases that have been used during the statement, explanation and illustration phases so that we connect them all. Let us return to the point from Matthew 24:36–44 that Jesus will come without warning. I might say something like, "Just as the weather on the hills can change without warning, so Jesus's return will be without warning. And just as the flood came on the people in Noah's day without further warning, so the Lord will return suddenly. Jesus will come without warning." The example I gave could be improved further by using "at a time you do not expect" instead of "without warning," because that is very close to the phrase Jesus uses in verse 44.

Using Biblical Stories and Cross References Properly

One of the reasons I was tempted to make the wrong point from Matthew 24 is that I know the passage in 2 Peter 2:4–5 which speaks of similar subjects. The apostle writes:

> For if God did not spare angels when they sinned, but sent them to hell, putting them in chains of darkness to be held for judgment; if he did not spare the ancient world when he brought the flood on its ungodly people, but protected Noah, a preacher of righteousness, and seven others . . .

Peter's opponents deny that God will in fact do anything about the false teachers. His reply is to say that just as God certainly acted in the case of Noah, so Jesus will certainly return to deal with these false teachers. Peter's point here is that Jesus's return is as *certain* as the flood that swept away Noah's generation. But in Matthew 24, Jesus leans on the story of Noah to show that the flood came *suddenly*, at least in the sense that there were no signs to warn people apart from Noah's preaching. It is true that the flood was both certain and sudden; and equally it is true that Jesus's return will be both certain and sudden. The process of finding the right explanatory story to explain and illustrate Matthew

24:36–44 showed me the importance of working to understand what is being said in *this passage*, which is that his return will be *sudden*. As we saw above, the challenge of fitting the explanatory story to the passage made me check that I had the right story *for the point being made in this passage.*

In expository preaching, our task is to explain just one passage only. In general, expository preaching aims to start in one passage and to stay in that passage. When we stop moving away from the passage and start digging into it, we invariably find that it is filled with treasure. With that said, there are times when it may be helpful to visit other parts of the Bible. I advise my preachers to do so with, as it were, elastic tied to their waists so that they are always drawn back to the starting passage! Let us look at some helpful and unhelpful uses of biblical cross references. They are labelled with a letter in order to tie in with the exercise that follows.

(A) Helpful Cross References That Can Help You to Understand Your Passage

The first type of helpful cross reference is where we need another part of the Bible to help us to understand the passage that we are preaching. We should at least look up the other passage in our preparation.

In Matthew 24:36–44, for example, we need at least to know the story of Noah (Gen 6–9) to understand Jesus's allusion to the days of Noah in verse 38. If a passage directly quotes another biblical passage we should look up the original passage to understand the quotation. In Matthew 8:17 we see Jesus healing many who had diseases, and Matthew explains, "This was to fulfil what was spoken through the prophet Isaiah: 'He took up our infirmities and bore our diseases.'" This quotes from Isaiah 53:4 in which Isaiah speaks of the Servant. Matthew wants us to see how Jesus fulfils the prophecy about the Servant. In a similar way, when Paul refers to Christ as our Passover lamb (1 Cor 5:7), he is taking us back to the Old Testament background such as Exodus 12. A cross reference is justified when it is needed in order to understand the passage.

Sometimes the story we are studying is continued elsewhere. For instance, when Rahab rescues the Israelite spies she extracts a promise that they will protect her house when the city is conquered (Josh 2:12–13). Later Joshua commands the spies to rescue Rahab and her family, keeping the promise they made (Josh 6:22–23). We need to look up the later passage to understand the earlier passage. Were we preaching on Joshua 6, we would also need to look up Joshua 2 – at least in our preparation.

(B) Helpful Cross-References That Can Help You to Apply Your Passage

Sometimes a cross reference is needed in order to apply the passage properly. This is often the case when a theme in the Old Testament is picked up in the New Testament. For example, if we are preaching from the story of the first Passover, Exodus 12 shows us how the Passover lambs died in place of the Israelite firstborn (see Exod 12:12–13). The application for Christians is not that we should kill a lamb or stay indoors: we need to know that this true story points to Jesus who is our Passover lamb, who died in place of each of us. The ultimate application of Exodus 12 is about our rescue from sin, not their rescue from slavery (see, for example, 1 Cor 5:7; John 1:29). Or if we preach on Rahab the prostitute who rescued the Israelite spies, we need to remember how her faith is commended in Hebrews 11:31 and James 2:25; and maybe also recall that she became one of Jesus's ancestors, according to Matthew 1:5. Finally the passage we preach may link to a larger biblical theme which we need to pick up in order to apply it correctly. For example, if a passage in the Old Testament speaks about the temple and the sacrificial system, we must connect to the New Testament's teaching that Jesus is the new temple and that because of his once-for-all sacrifice there is no longer any sacrifice for sin.

(C) Helpful Cross-References That Can Help You to Illustrate Your Passage

Next, we can use a cross reference if it illustrates the point being made. The Bible has many little stories which can be helpful in explaining our passage and in preaching. The houses in my town have walls and windows. The walls are stronger than the windows, so if I were to remove a window, the wind and rain would come in but the house would still stand. The windows are not load-bearing. If the house is a metaphor for our sermon, then the windows stand for explanatory stories. And just as I should be able to take windows out of my house without causing it to fall, so we should be able to take the explanatory stories out of our sermon without causing it to fall. It will not be as clear but it will still be as true.

Now what if our little story is taken from the Bible rather than from daily life? If we can remove that cross reference and our point still stands, then it is being used to illustrate. If, however, the point changes when we take out the second biblical reference, it is clear that we are depending on the cross reference to make our point. If we are using the reference to help with understanding (category A) or with application (B) then that may be legitimate. But otherwise we should return to the passage we are preaching and make the point from there only. We can use Bible images and stories to illustrate our passage if they are genuinely being used as explanatory stories and not as an excuse to avoid expounding the text before us. For example, in his letter to Titus, Paul refers to God as our "Saviour."[1] A saviour is someone who rescues another. I could illustrate this using real-life rescues; or I could illustrate by telling the story of rescues in the Bible: how God rescued Jacob's family from famine through Joseph; or how God rescued Israel from the Egyptian armies; or how Rahab rescued the spies, and then God rescued Rahab through the spies; or how God rescued Shadrach, Meshach and Abednego from the fiery furnace, or Daniel from the lions' den.[2] I do not *need* any of these stories to make the point that God is a saviour and rescuer: but each of these stories can help explain the point.

(X) Unhelpful Cross References Where the Idea Is Similar but Not Similar Enough

We turn now to three unhelpful ways to use cross references in expository preaching. First, in Matthew 24:38, Jesus mentions Noah to make the point that his return will be *sudden*. In 2 Peter 2:5 the mention of Noah makes the point that Jesus's return is *certain*. The two passages make different points from the same event, as we saw above. For that reason I think that 2 Peter 2:5 would be an unhelpful cross reference when preaching on Matthew 24:38 (and also the other way round). I remember hearing a sermon on Colossians in which the preacher said, "I'm not sure what Paul means here, but he uses the same words in a different letter which I think is a bit easier, so I will speak about that instead." At that point he abandoned faithfulness to the text. Please do not imitate him!

A more extreme example might be to compare the New Testament comment for husbands to love their wives as Christ loved the church (Eph 5:25) with the second great commandment to love your neighbour as yourself (Lev 19:18 and Matt 22:39, among many other references). Both are commands to show love and care to other people. But it is as wrong to love your wife as a mere neighbour as it would be to show your neighbour the kind of love reserved for your wife! The idea is about loving other people, but the differences in meaning are too important to miss.

---

1. The word is used three times of God and three times of Christ: Titus 1:3–4; 2:10, 13; 3:4, 6.

2. Gen 42–47; Exod 14; Josh 2; 6; Dan 3; 6.

(Y) Unhelpful Cross References Where the Word Is Similar but the Context Is Not

One passage may pick up the same word or phrase as another but that does not mean they are linked in a way that will help us to teach the truth. For example, Rahab tied a scarlet cord to her window so that the spies would know her house when they returned. The midwife who delivered Tamar's twins also tied a scarlet cord around the wrist of Zerah. Isaiah says that Israel's guilt and the pardon that God promises are as different as scarlet wool and white snow. When Jesus was mocked he was clothed in a scarlet robe.[3] The word "scarlet" links all four references but the contexts are different in every case. In the first two the colour of the thread is not that significant – the story would still be true if blue or yellow thread had been used. In the third story Isaiah relies on the sharp contrast between scarlet and white, while in the last scarlet was the colour of military tunics. This is just word association: we are never told that Rahab used scarlet thread because she was especially sinful. If we use word studies or searches we must be careful always to look up the context of the cross reference and ask whether there is really any connection with our passage. The cross references in our Bibles may even link us to an associated word: but that does not mean it is right to rest on it for preaching.

(Z) Unhelpful Cross References Where the Action Is Similar but the Context Is Not

As well as word-association links there are action-association links. Rahab helped the spies escape by letting them down the city wall on a rope.[4] My Bible gives a cross reference to Acts 9:25, where the disciples help Saul escape from Damascus by lowering him down a city wall in a basket. That helps me as a reader when I think, "Isn't there another time someone escapes from a city like that?," but it does not help me with preaching. The spies in Jericho and Saul in Damascus were on completely different missions and were rescued with different promises. Rahab will not help us preach Acts 9; nor will Paul's story in Damascus help us with the spies in Jericho. The only connection is that they were lowered down a wall.

In conclusion then, biblical cross references are sometimes necessary in order to understand the passage or to apply the passage. They can also be used to illustrate a passage, but this must be done with caution. And biblical

---

3. Josh 2:18; Gen 38:27–30; Isa 1:18; Matt 27:28.
4. Josh 2:15.

cross references should be avoided if they do not help us understand, apply or illustrate the point.

Exercise

Identify which type of cross reference is being used in each of the passages below, using the letters A, B, C, X, Y or Z:

- (A) Required to *understand* the passage properly.
- (B) Required to *apply* the passage properly.
- (C) *Illustrates* the point being made from your passage.
- (X) Unhelpful: a similar idea but not similar enough.
- (Y) Unhelpful: word association.
- (Z) Unhelpful: action association.

Passages:

- Matthew 27:46 and Psalm 22:1
- Luke 22:37 and Isaiah 53:12
- Matthew 1:20 and Genesis 37:5
- Matthew 1:23 and Isaiah 7:14
- Matthew 8:4 and Leviticus 14:2–32
- Mark 9:40 and Matthew 12:30
- Luke 7:11–17 and 1 Kings 17:17–24
- Luke 15:3–7 and Matthew 15:24

Analysis

Matthew 27:46 and Psalm 22:1 (A, B). When Jesus takes Psalm 22 on his lips, it is both a commentary and an explanation of his suffering. We need to read the psalm in order to understand the gospel and maybe also to apply it. It's A and maybe B.

Luke 22:37 and Isaiah 53:12 (A). Luke connects Jesus's treatment as a criminal with the Servant's role of being numbered with sinners (transgressors). We need to understand Isaiah's prophecy about the Servant in order to understand the death of Jesus. So it's A, needed for understanding.

Matthew 1:20 and Genesis 37:5 (Y). In both passages, Joseph has a dream. But it's not the same Joseph and not the same dream. So it's Y, unhelpful word association.

Matthew 1:23 and Isaiah 7:14 (A). The New Testament passage directly quotes the other, which is needed in order to understand Matthew 1:23.

Matthew 8:4 and Leviticus 14:2–32 (A). Jesus tells the cleansed leper to present himself to the priest, according to rites described in Leviticus 14.

Mark 9:40 and Matthew 12:30 (X). In Mark 9:40, Jesus says that "whoever is not against us is for us." The parallel saying in Matthew is similar: "whoever is not with me is against me, and whoever does not gather with me scatters." This is X, where the idea is similar but not similar enough to be saying the same thing. Each passage needs to be understood in its own context.

Luke 7:11–17 and 1 Kings 17:17–24 (possible A, Z and maybe C). Jesus's healing of the widow's son recalls Elijah's healing of the widow's son. The parallels between the two healings may suggest that Jesus fulfils a type that Elijah foreshadowed, in which case we need the cross reference to understand the passage (A). On the other hand, we do not need Elijah's story to understand Jesus's miracle because Luke is already painting the picture of Jesus's authority, which would mean it's a type Z cross reference.

Luke 15:3–7 and Matthew 15:24 (X or Y). The idea of the lost sheep is common to both passages but used in totally different ways, so the connection is unhelpful, whether it's a false word association (Y) or action association (Z).

In summary, then, explanatory stories need a point to explain. The point needs to be clear in our minds before we look for a little story. Sometimes the passage itself has enough images; at other times a story from everyday life can be effective. Cross references from the Bible can also be used, but with caution. In the next chapter we will see how to use explanatory stories even better.

For Further Reading

Crowter, Phil. *Preaching God's Big Story: Talk Outlines for a Bible Overview.* London: The Good Book Company, 2008.

(More detailed) Goldsworthy, Graeme. *Preaching the Whole Bible as Christian Scripture: The Application of Biblical Theology to Expository Preaching.* Leicester: IVP, 2000.

Meynell, Mark. *What Angels Long to Read: Reading and Preaching the New Testament.* Carlisle: Langham Preaching Resources, 2017, especially chapter 1 and appendix 4.

Wright, Christopher J. H. *Sweeter Than Honey: Preaching the Old Testament.* Carlisle: Langham Preaching Resources, 2015, especially chapter 5, "Connecting with Christ."

3

Make Explanatory Stories Work Even Better

Explanatory stories work best when used to make a point. They work even better when the point they illustrate lines up exactly with the point being made from the passage. This section shares ideas to make explanatory stories work even better still.

Add Just Enough Detail

When we tell stories, we owe it to our hearers to use their time well. That means using no more detail than necessary. Biblical writers are sparing with details. Consider, for instance, the few details we have in Nathan's parable in 2 Samuel 12. We are told that the rich man had a very large number of sheep and cattle, in contrast to the poor man who had "nothing except one little ewe lamb that he had bought. He raised it, and it grew up with him and his children. It shared his food, drank from his cup and even slept in his arms. It was like a daughter to him" (2 Sam 12:3). We do not need to know how many animals the rich man owned, nor where he grazed them, nor who cared for his flocks and herds, nor what breed of beast they were. But we do need to know about the poor man's one ewe lamb and how deeply he cared for it. Nathan gives us just enough detail to feel the shock of what happens next.

Flooding, Forgetting and Failing to Resolve

We let our hearers down when we flood them with detail, forget details or fail to resolve the stories we use.

I told the story in the previous chapter of Sir Ernest Shackleton's ill-fated journey to the South Pole. I recently visited an exhibition of photographs and was pleased to find a picture of the whole crew, with their names written below. I was amazed to see the last entry: "Perce Blackborow, stowaway (later steward)." I wonder what Perce thought about his decision to sneak aboard as he sat on Elephant Island, surviving on seal meat and blubber for weeks on end while they waited in expectation for their leader to return. It is a fascinating detail! But it is utterly irrelevant to my purpose in telling about Shackleton, which was to give an explanatory story about how the men were confident of being rescued. This detail will not help us to explain the point. I might consider telling people about Perce if I felt we needed a breather or if there is some reason why this story makes a local connection; perhaps Perce Blackborow originally came from the town I am preaching in.

If we forget details and have to interrupt the story to add new information we will probably annoy our hearers. Just as when someone on the phone puts you on hold to speak with another caller, it feels impolite. Thankfully the remedy is simple: we need to rehearse or write out our stories before we tell them so that we include all the necessary details at the right points.

A third mistake is to fail to resolve plots in the story. John Chapman gives an example involving the story of a fifteen-year-old unlicensed driver who ran into Chapman's car causing significant damage. In order for the car to be fixed, someone had to pay for it: either Chapman could let the boy off and pay for the damage himself, or he could confront the boy's father and see if he would make good; or he could go to the police in order to have the boy charged and then he could file an insurance claim. The point of the story was to illustrate that when God forgives sin, there is a price to be paid, and that price is paid by Jesus on the cross. But Chapman comments:

> When I used this illustration I was regularly asked the question, "What did you do with the boy?" The story was too vivid and opened up other complex issues such that the death of Jesus was forgotten in this real life drama of the teenager and the car. It was fun while it lasted but useless as an illustration.[1]

---

1. John Chapman, *Setting Hearts on Fire: A Guide to Giving Evangelistic Talks* (NSW, Australia: Matthias Media, 1999), 108.

Every Detail Has a Purpose

Some apparently irrelevant details can have purpose. For instance, all four gospels tell the miracle of the feeding of the five thousand and mention that the people sat down to eat; three gospels mention there was grass, and Mark 6:39 tells us the grass was green (Matt 14:13–23; Mark 6:30–46; Luke 9:10–17; John 6:1–15). As far as I can tell, neither the grass nor its colour has a direct bearing on the miracle or what follows. So why did the evangelists include it? I think it is because the grass is an eyewitness detail included to show the credibility of their sources. We will see later that motivational stories need credible details, and the green grass is a credible detail: there may not be grass all year round in that part of the world, and to state that the grass was green places the miracle in a specific season.[2] The gospel writers were selective in what they included. John, for instance, tells us what guided his selection: "Jesus performed many other signs in the presence of his disciples, which are not recorded in this book. But these are written that you may believe that Jesus is the Messiah, the Son of God, and that by believing you may have life in his name" (John 20:30–31).

Sometimes we can give more details than strictly necessary if we believe doing so will help our hearers trust the message. This might be by giving some facts; or by showing why the person being quoted is an authority; or even to show that this is a story about someone connected to that place – I might say that I had been chatting with so-and-so who lives in this very village; or that this person was a professor at that university: it depends on what would make a connection with our critical or questioning listener. Let us make every detail count; and what counts depends on our context.

Make a Better Connection with the Passage

As well as getting the level of detail right, a second area of attention to make little stories work harder is to make the link between the point and the image as clear as possible. We saw that the explanatory story is like a flag planted on the summit of the point. The clearer the point, the better the fit can be between image and point.

We can pick up words and ideas that are in the passage or lie just below the surface. Here is an important verse for Bible teachers: "Do your best to present yourself to God as one approved, a worker who does not need to be ashamed and who correctly handles the word of truth" (2 Tim 2:15). A literal

---

2. Peter J. Williams, *Can We Trust the Gospels?* (Wheaton, IL: Crossway, 2018), 91, refers to this as an undesigned coincidence.

translation of the word behind "correctly handles" is "to cut straight." If we can identify the grain of a passage, we can divide it into the right sections.

I sometimes illustrate this further by telling the story of the first time I tried to cut a mango. I am familiar with apples and oranges, which can be cut in almost any direction, but mangoes cannot. When I began to cut a mango as I would an apple, it soon turned into a mess. My Kenyan host leaned over and expertly wielded the knife to divide the soft flesh from the husk. Because he knew the shape and texture of a mango, he could "correctly handle" the fruit, which meant cutting it properly. In a similar way, when we know the shape and texture of a biblical passage, we can correctly handle the word of truth and get a feel for the ideas and images in the passage that can be picked up in the explanatory story. Then we can confidently use a story that describes the same kind of event that the text is speaking about.

Consider the passage where Jesus says, "I will ask the Father, and he will give you another advocate to help you and be with you forever – the Spirit of truth" (John 14:16–17). It is helpful to know that the word "another" used here (*allos*) means "another of the same kind." There is a different Greek word (*heteros*) which means "another of a different kind." I would look for a little story that illustrates the idea of another of the same kind. For example, pastor Graham Beynon tells this story:

> I've got an identical twin brother. We really are very alike, not only in appearance, but also, so people say, in our mannerisms and expressions. When we visit each other, all kinds of confusion are caused among friends we meet! Now if I were leaving my church, I could say to the congregation, "I'm going, but I'll send another Graham." Obviously they might like to ask for something different but you see the point. I could promise another one just like me, to take my place.

He then connects his story back to the passage by using the same terms:

> That's what Jesus is promising here – another helper to be with them, to take his place. The Holy Spirit and Jesus are so similar that Jesus can speak about coming to them, or later he can say he'll be with them for ever (Matthew 28:20).[3]

---

3. Graham Beynon, *Experiencing the Spirit: New Testament Essentials for Every Christian* (Nottingham: IVP, 2006), 28.

Make a Better Connection with the People and Their Emotions

Preaching is God's work. Paul thanks God that when the church at Thessalonica heard his message, they accepted it "not as a human word, but as it actually is, the word of God, which is indeed at work in you who believe" (1 Thess 2:13). Our role as preachers is to do all we can to bring that word to human hearts so that it becomes what James calls "the word planted in you, which can save you" (Jas 1:21). What follows are ideas to plant that word deep in our hearers' hearts.

Engage Head, Heart and Hands

Our work as Bible *teachers* is to enable *learning*, but that is not enough. Our goal as *preachers* is life *transformation*. We can spot the difference by looking at a sermon's aim sentence.[4] Let us return to Matthew 24:36–44. My theme sentence was "Jesus warned the disciples to be ready because his return would be sudden." My aim sentence is "We should always be ready because Jesus's return will be sudden." I can make my aim sentence more precise:

- I believe that God wants my hearers to *know* that Jesus is coming suddenly.
- I believe that God wants my hearers to *get ready* for Jesus's return.
- I believe that God wants my hearers to *long* for Jesus's return.

Let us think about the kind of change we are looking for with each of these aims. The goal of *knowing* that Jesus will return suddenly is primarily one of *information*. When the hearers can repeat that new information back to me, I think they have probably understood this – in their heads. Transformation begins when understanding changes the way they *think* and *act*. That is why the second aim sentence is stronger: I want my hearers to *get ready*. They will need to move from inaction to action, from unreadiness to readiness. This sermon demands action, and that inevitably engages the hands as well as the head. The final aim sentence engages the heart: in desiring my hearers to *long* for Jesus's return, the head is engaged because I know he is coming; the heart is engaged because I am emotionally tied in to this truth; and therefore the hands will follow. It is fair to say that our sermon applications should always be asking what this passage wants us to think, do or feel. If we are preaching for transformative learning, we need to engage the whole person, which means

---

4. The aim sentence for a sermon summarizes what, under God, we want our hearers to do as a result of the sermon. The theme sentence, as usually understood in preaching seminars, summarizes what the passage is about.

reaching the will through the heart. We saw above how this corresponds to Augustine's ancient categories of informing, delighting and moving hearers.

Engage the Emotions in the Way You Tell Stories

Words evoke images in the mind. Everything we have done above is intended to help us to paint a picture before the hearers. We want them to *see*. Some people learn better using their other senses and we can include them in the way that we tell the story. We can describe the smell, taste and emotions of the story as well as simply painting a picture in words. When telling of Shackleton's rescue, for example, we can describe the conditions the men faced in their long anxious wait on Elephant Island: the men, the dogs, the dirt, and the all-pervading smell of fish and seal oil, their main diet. (Seals smell – strongly – of fish!) We keep the details down to what is needed, but if they engage the senses they are adding credible detail. These make the story real to the listeners.

Humour can make a strong emotional connection with people. This is helpful with those who do not know us or may not trust us, for example in an evangelistic setting. Humour can also get past our defences by highlighting things in the world that do not fit together, which is often why we find them funny. John Stott comments that "humour can be a preparation for the gospel. Since it can contribute to the awakening within human hearts of shame over what we are and longing for what we could be, we should press it gladly into the cause of the gospel."[5] But it needs to be used with caution. Jesus used humour to make his teaching memorable and clear, but he never used it to hurt or harm others.

Use Active Elements

A visual aid can also help. I recently heard someone explain John 12:24: "Very truly I tell you, unless a grain of wheat falls to the ground and dies, it remains only a single seed. But if it dies, it produces many seeds." As well as *telling* us about the seed and the fruitlessness of a seed that is not buried in the ground, the speaker *showed* us a packet of seeds. This small step helped us make a visual connection between the seeds and the point Jesus is making. We often naturally use active elements when teaching children. To illustrate this passage

---

5. John R. W. Stott and Greg Scharf, *The Challenge of Preaching* (Carlisle: Langham Preaching Resources, 2011), 77–78. See also Stott, *I Believe in Preaching*, 292.

for young people, we might sow a seed one week and see what has happened by the next. (I am told that cress seeds grow helpfully fast!)

More than this, we can add simple actions that will reinforce our point. The following are examples in which the preacher uses the Bible as a prop.

First, I remember clearly when Isaiah 53:6 was first explained to me:

> We all, like sheep, have gone astray,
>> each of us has turned to our own way;
> and the LORD has laid on him
>> the iniquity of us all.

The speaker held both hands palm upwards. He told us that his right hand represented Jesus Christ, whose life was in unbroken fellowship with God, symbolized by an open hand with nothing between him and God above. The speaker's left hand represented my life, burdened by sin that was symbolized by a Bible which blocked the way between my life and God above. That illustrated the first part of the verse: "We all, like sheep, have gone astray, each of us has turned to our own way." As the speaker recited the second part of the verse, he transferred the book from his left hand (me) to his right hand (Jesus): "and the LORD has laid on *him* the iniquity of us all." He then asked, "Where is your sin now?" "On Jesus," came the reply. I understood what had happened when Jesus died on the cross in my place, and why this means I can now have fellowship with God. The speaker could have described the story as I have done in words here, but the fact that I could see the explanatory story acted out, and indeed could hear the words spoken, drove the story – and the truth it explains – deeper into my heart. It's a very simple image made more powerful by being active. And all it needs is a Bible, which the speaker should have anyway!

A second example helps explain the significance of being "in Christ." In Ephesians, Paul explains that a Christian believer is united or joined to Christ by faith. This is not by our own efforts because without Christ we can only be described as spiritually dead: "As for you, you were dead in your transgressions and sins, in which you used to live when you followed the ways of this world and of the ruler of the kingdom of the air, the spirit who is now at work in those who are disobedient" (Eph 2:1–2).

Paul makes clear in the next verses that he too was in the same situation. The wonderful news of God's grace and love breaks out in verses 4 and 5: "But because of his great love for us, God, who is rich in mercy, made us alive with Christ even when we were dead in transgressions – it is by grace you have been saved." And there is more in verses 6–7: "And God raised us up with Christ and seated us with him in the heavenly realms in Christ Jesus, in order that in the coming ages he might show the incomparable riches of his grace, expressed in his kindness to us in Christ Jesus."

When Jesus ascended, he sat down at the right hand of the Father. And here is the amazing bit: *we are seated with him*! We see this from the repeated phrase "with Christ": "And God raised us up *with Christ* and seated us *with him* in the heavenly realms *in Christ Jesus*" (v. 6). When we are "in Christ," what is true of Christ becomes true of us. He died to sin and we died with him; he was raised and God raised us with him; and he is seated and God seated us with him. The way I saw this illustrated was when the preacher took a piece of paper and slipped it into his Bible. When he lifted the book, the paper was lifted too. When he lowered the book, the paper was lowered too, because it was "in the book." In a similar way, when we are "in Christ" who is seated at God's right hand, we too are lifted up and seated there. The application is a simple one when it is described: when it is performed, it becomes powerful and memorable.

A final example comes from a young persons' summer camp. The talks were all taken from the book of Exodus and the stage was set with three lecterns spaced apart in a row at the front of the stage. The first was labelled "Egypt," the second "New Testament Times" and the last "Today." These were the three horizons for teaching the passages, first according to the context in Exodus, then according to its meaning for the New Testament, and finally how it applies to life today. It was a very simple visual way of representing the important steps involved in taking the message from the text to today: we need to ask what it meant to the original people (Egypt); how it is fulfilled in the New Testament; and finally what it means for us today. It is no surprise that the most gifted youth and children's workers are brilliant at engaging all the senses – head, heart and hands – in their Bible teaching.

Use Visual Aids, Music and Pictures

Screens and projectors can make using visual aids much easier. We do not need to be able to paint like Rembrandt if we can project a photo of his masterful painting "The Return of the Prodigal Son," for example. We can play a piece of music through a computer, phone or tablet; we can show a video clip. All these can be powerful – if used well. The key should be obvious by now: once we are *really clear* on what we wish the visual aid to do, we can evaluate whether this will work. A painting of the returning son, for example, helps us to *feel* the father's love for his child – provided that seventeenth-century Western art connects with our hearers. A video clip may help us enter into the experience of being lost – or whatever point we are trying to make. Using the categories we have developed above – explanatory stories for illumination, motivational stories for motivation, exemplary stories for application – we can judge whether our visual aid, picture, song or video clip will make a better connection with our hearers *for that purpose.* Remember when using visual aids that some of your hearers may be visually impaired and unable to see the visual aid. It does not take much to learn the simple discipline of briefly describing what you want people to see: it means a lot to those who are included because you have taken the trouble to do this.

If a little story can be enhanced by adding an active ingredient, why not use a concrete object rather than a picture painted with words? Visual aids can be very powerful if they are well chosen and fit exactly with the point being made. A plant clinging to a crack in a paving stone is a striking image and yet so simple.[6]

In using objects we are limited by what can be found in real life. We can *show* a packet of seeds, but we need to *tell* of Yellowstone, or Shackleton, or even the hillwalkers. But if an object can be found, the impact can be great. One friend of mine uses a funeral wreath to teach the truth that Jesus defeated the power of death when he rose from the grave. At the point in his talk when he explains that death has been defeated, my friend smashes the wreath on the ground, where it breaks into several pieces. The shock of breaking something related to funerals engages the heart and sticks in the mind.

We can add action to make the visual aid more powerful. For example, I sometimes teach the story of the first Passover from Exodus 12 by creating a door frame. As I tell how the Israelites were told to slaughter a lamb and "take a bunch of hyssop, dip it into the blood in the basin and put some of the blood on the top and on both sides of the door-frame" (Exod 12:22), I put red paint on the top and both sides of our own door frame. This connects the Israelites' trust in the blood of the Passover lamb with our trust in the blood of Jesus who is our Passover Lamb (1 Cor 5:7).

A simple diagram that grows as you explain it is far more powerful than a complex handout. This is because the explanation takes place *around* the diagram through the actions and words of the speaker. I know of one speaker whose talk about preaching is entitled "Above the line and below the line." The only picture he draws is of a horizontal line, and that appears only midway through the talk. The speaker talks about the line long before he draws it, which makes us hunger for the line long before it appears.

---

6. See the section "Be Alert" in chapter 6.

Sometimes an action can make a personal response more concrete. Evangelist Billy Graham used to ask those who wanted to trust in Christ to leave their seats and come to the front of the hall: he was inviting them to make visible the step of commitment they had made in their hearts. At a simple level we can ask our hearers to write down one action they will take this week as a result of the sermon. This invites everyone to make a personal response, and requires them to think what this means for them.[7]

Whatever we do, the visual aid or action must fit exactly with the purpose it serves in exactly the same way as the explanatory, motivational or exemplary story. And we should remember that visual aids can let us down. That is why it is a good idea to make sure that the talk will work even if the visual aid collapses, or we leave it behind, or we have to preach through a power cut.

Fit the Stories to the Setting

Finally, we need to ensure that the stories we use are appropriate for the people we are speaking to. This is especially important if we give the same talk in different settings. Although the theme and aim sentences will be unchanged, we should think about changing the stories that we use when giving the same talk in different settings. When ministry is busy I try to double up on preparation as much as possible: I might preach a passage on a Sunday morning in my own church; preach the same in a neighbouring church that has very different people attending; give a talk from the same passage to the children at school during the week; use the passage as the basis of a devotional for a staff meeting or a Christian committee meeting; and share it with the seniors' midweek meeting. Provided there aren't too many people who hear the talk more than once, it's a legitimate way to make full use of a passage that is on my heart. But although I can use the same *passage*, I cannot use the same *talk* – at least, not without adjustment. And the chief adjustments will be in the stories I tell: I am unlikely to be able to use the same stories for the midweek seniors that I use for the devotional or the schoolchildren.

Exercise

Think of three different settings in which you might be called on to give a talk. Take your most recent talk: which stories would you need to adapt or change? What alternatives can you think of?

---

7. See Langham Helps #49 and #56–58 for more on using active responses in training: Langham Partnership, *Helps*, vol. 2, 15, 24–26.

To summarise, an explanatory story is a word picture that can bring understanding by making the abstract more concrete and the remote more immediate. We can make our stories work better by paying attention to the details and by engaging all the senses.

For Further Reading

Chapman, John. *Setting Hearts on Fire: A Guide to Giving Evangelistic Talks*. NSW: Matthias Media, 1999.

Stott, John R. W., and Greg Scharf. *The Challenge of Preaching*. Carlisle: Langham Preaching Resources, 2011.

4

Tell Motivational Stories for Action

A second kind of little story is the motivational story. While explanatory stories help us to understand, motivational stories help us to be *moved to act*. We can see the different uses of explanatory and motivational stories by thinking about where in the point we are making we use them. If an image or story is primarily for illumination (explanatory story) then we would tie it to the "validate and explain" phase of making the point. By contrast, a story that needs to *motivate* the hearers is usually linked to the application stage.

The most common type of motivational story is the narrative because a story with a plot, suspense and resolution engages the emotions powerfully. According to Chip and Dan Heath, a story has power to do two things: to provide knowledge about something to act (stimulation) and to give motivation to act (inspiration). When both benefits are present they generate action: "a *credible* idea makes people believe. An *emotional* idea makes people care."[1] In the right hands, such stories are great tools. They are stories that serve.

Telling the Story Well

At its simplest a good story has an introduction, descriptive details, movement through crisis and a conclusion. "Crisis" has a specific meaning in this context and means a problem that listeners have an interest in solving. As with an explanatory story we need to link the motivational story with the teaching point. The punchline of our story must line up with the point being made

---

1. Chip Heath and Dan Heath, *Made to Stick: Why Some Ideas Survive and Others Die* (New York: Random House, 2007), 206.

from the passage, if possible using similar words and phrases. As an example, consider the following stories:

A Cut to the Heart Saves a King's Life

> There were two men in a certain town, one rich and the other poor. The rich man had a very large number of sheep and cattle, but the poor man had nothing except one little ewe lamb he had bought. He raised it, and it grew up with him and his children. It shared his food, drank from his cup and even slept in his arms. It was like a daughter to him.
>
> Now a traveller came to the rich man, but the rich man refrained from taking one of his own sheep or cattle to prepare a meal for the traveller who had come to him. Instead, he took the ewe lamb that belonged to the poor man and prepared it for the one who had come to him. (2 Sam 12:1–4)

How does this story make you *feel*? Even this brief telling makes us care about the poor man whose only ewe lamb was taken from him: we surely feel anger at the injustice. When King David was told this parable by the prophet Nathan, he felt anger: "David burned with anger against the man and said to Nathan, 'As surely as the LORD lives, the man who did this must die! He must pay for that lamb four times over, because he did such a thing and had no pity'" (2 Sam 12:5–6).

David's anger was the opening for God's word to enter his hard heart. David's heart had been closed to God through his refusal to acknowledge his sin when he slept with Bathsheba and conspired to murder her husband Uriah. Nathan makes the connection between the story and the sinner:

> Then Nathan said to David, "You are the man! This is what the LORD, the God of Israel, says: 'I anointed you king over Israel, and I delivered you from the hand of Saul. I gave your master's house to you, and your master's wives into your arms. I gave you all Israel and Judah. And if all this had been too little, I would have given you even more. Why did you despise the word of the LORD by doing what is evil in his eyes? You struck down Uriah the Hittite with the sword and took his wife to be your own. You killed him with the sword of the Ammonites. Now, therefore, the sword shall never depart from your house, because you despised me and took the wife of Uriah the Hittite to be your own.'" (2 Sam 12:7–10)

David is touched by Nathan's parable, and then cut to the heart. We can see how Nathan has used a moving story to make David *feel* the truth. And because David feels the truth, he will now act: he is cut to the heart – and repents. Here is a motivational story which acts on the heart to produce action.

A Stab in the Heart Saves a Baby's Life

The second example is deliberately chosen from outside the Bible, to demonstrate that this use of stories draws on universal wisdom.

> The nurse was working in the neonatal intensive-care unit, where newborns with serious health problems are treated and monitored. She'd been watching one baby in particular for several hours, and she didn't like what she was seeing. His color, a key indicator of potential problems, had been fluctuating – wavering between a healthy shade of pink and a duller, more troublesome hue.
>
> Suddenly, within a matter of seconds, the baby turned a deep blue-black. The nurse's stomach fell. Others in the ICU yelled for an X-ray technician and a doctor.
>
> The gathering medical team was operating on the assumption that the baby's lung had collapsed, a common problem for babies on ventilators. The team prepared for the typical response to a collapsed lung, which involves piercing the chest and inserting a tube to suck the air from around the collapsed lung, allowing it to reinflate.
>
> But the nurse thought it was a heart problem. As soon as she saw the baby's color – that awful blue-black – she suspected a pneumopericardium, a condition in which air fills the sac surrounding the heart, pressing inward and preventing the heart from beating. The nurse was terrified, because the last time she witnessed a pneumopericardium the baby died before the problem could even be diagnosed.
>
> The nurse tried to stop the frantic preparations to treat the lung. "It's the heart!" she said. But in response the other medical personnel pointed to the heart monitors, which showed that the baby's heart was fine; his heart rate was bouncing along steadily, at the normal newborn rate of 130 beats per minute. The nurse, still insistent, pushed their hands away and screamed for quiet as she lowered a stethoscope to check for a heartbeat.

There was no sound – the heart was not beating.

She started doing compressions on the baby's chest. The chief neonatologist burst into the room and the nurse slapped a syringe in his hand. "It's a pneumopericardium," she said. "Stick the heart."

The X-ray technician, who was finally receiving results from his scan, confirmed the nurse's diagnosis. The neonatologist guided the syringe into the heart and slowly released the air that had been strangling the baby's heart. The baby's life was saved. His color slowly returned to normal.

Later, the group realized why the heart monitor had misled them. It is designed to measure electrical activity, not actual heartbeats. The baby's heart nerves were firing – telling the heart to beat at the appropriate rate – but the air in the sac around the heart prevented the heart from actually beating. Only when the nurse used the stethoscope – so she could hear whether the heart was pumping correctly – did it become clear that his heart had stopped.[2]

As a story, this is moving and maybe a bit long for a sermon. But notice how it works: there are credible details, but not too many; there is a clear crisis; there are characters whom we care about; and when the resolution comes we are mightily relieved.

What kind of point would this story illustrate in a sermon? The key to finding the point of a story is to look for the turning point, the part of the story when the situation starts to turn from bad to good. The crisis was that the baby was being treated for the wrong condition, a collapsed lung rather than air in the sac around the heart. The turning point was the nurse's persistence in calling for quiet so that she could listen to the heart with a stethoscope. Although the baby did not begin to get better until the paediatrician gave the injection, it was the nurse's diagnosis that turned the situation around: "It's a story about a woman who stuck to her guns, despite implicit pressure to conform to the group's opinion."[3] The point of the story, then, is to learn from the nurse who persisted in what she believed was right. If we use this story as the motivational story in a sermon, it should be to encourage our hearers to keep doing what is right, even if they are alone.

---

2. Heath and Heath, *Made to Stick*, 204–5.

3. Heath and Heath, 206.

Exercise

In preaching Matthew 24:36–44 we will want to make the point that Jesus will come without warning. How do you think the people of Noah's generation, the men in the field or the women in the mill (Matt 24:38–41) *felt* when the terrible events came upon them without warning? Can you think of a story that describes a person who feels the same way? Could you use this story to connect your hearers to that experience, so that the truth of Jesus's unannounced return becomes real to them?

_____

_____

_____

Two Final Warnings

A carpenter quickly learns that sharp tools can make for good work. They cut accurately through wood. Sharp tools can also easily cut through flesh. That is why a skilled worker uses his or her tools with respect. In the same way, motivational stories are sharp words that can be used to build or to injure. We use their power with care and respect, because others may not. False teachers will use every means at their disposal to turn people away from the truth and tell people what their itching ears are waiting to hear (2 Tim 4:3). Most will use motivational stories, and some will use them very skilfully. So let us be careful to use these powerful tools in the service of the truth. We can do this better when we clearly align the point that the story is making with the point of the passage. We can also do this by ensuring that the story we are using is a little story, the servant of the passage. Remember that big stories tend to swallow up the sermon. If we use them in preaching, the danger is that we twist the passage to make it serve the moral of the big story.

That is why, second, we must not forget that the true power in preaching comes from the word of God itself. It is alive, active and sharper than any double-edged sword, achieving the purpose for which God sends it (Heb 4:12; Isa 55:10–11). The word is already powerful and does not need rhetorical help. As Augustine colourfully puts it in *On Christian Teaching*: "Just because it marches into battle without embellishment or armour, and apparently defenceless, this does not prevent it from crushing the enemy with the strength of its sinewy hands and disabling its opponent and demolishing falsehood with its mighty limbs."[4]

As preachers we use stories, and indeed all the means at our disposal, to bring that powerful word past the defences of the heart and mind. That is what the prophet Nathan did with hard-hearted King David.

For Further Reading

Chapell, Bryan. *Christ-Centered Preaching: Redeeming the Expository Sermon*, 2nd rev. ed. Grand Rapids, MI: Baker Academic, 2005. Chapters 7 and 8.

Heath, Chip, and Dan Heath. *Made to Stick: Why Some Ideas Survive and Others Die*. New York: Random House, 2007.

---

4. Augustine, *On Christian Teaching*, 141.

5

Use Exemplary Stories for Application

Learning to Tie a Knot

How did you learn to tie a knot, maybe to tie shoelaces? It is much easier to show someone how to tie a knot than to describe it using only words. It is the same with cooking, baking and many other crafts: it is easier to show than only to tell. It is also the same with discipleship in practice. We begin to follow Jesus through understanding – understanding our need of a saviour and understanding that Jesus is that saviour. Faith means turning from life on our own terms (we call this repentance) and bearing the fruit of practical Christian living. We now know what we want to do, but how to go about it? What does it look like in practice, and in my context? Practical examples put flesh on the bones of applying biblical teaching and this chapter will look at exemplary stories.

We have seen already that explanatory stories and motivational stories need to fit the context that we are speaking in: this is all the more true when it comes to exemplary stories because they will help our hearers to see what it looks like to walk as a follower of Jesus *in this place and time*, in other words in this culture. For that reason the examples given here can only be suggestions or pointers to what you will need to find and use in order to serve your people. This chapter is shorter because *only you* can provide the ending! You may know the saying that if you give a person a fish they have food for a day, but if you teach a person how to fish, they have food for life. This book aims for the same in using little stories: not to give you a stock of stories (giving you fish) but rather to show you how to make, find and use stories (how to fish). If I may extend the metaphor, I hope to give you a hook and line rather than a packet of fish. Which means that you need to finish the task by catching your own fish. That is why the chapters in the second part of this book are shorter: it is part of handing the task over to you.

The Thorn in the Flesh

Paul's thorn in the flesh is a practical example that helps us understand the biblical teaching that when we are weak, then we are strong. This is easier to say than to understand so Paul gives us a practical example from his experience: "Therefore, in order to keep me from becoming conceited, I was given a thorn in my flesh, a messenger of Satan, to torment me. Three times I pleaded with the Lord to take it away from me" (2 Cor 12:7–8).

We do not know what this thorn actually was. It may have been a physical illness, or perhaps a mental illness. But we do know that Paul faced this "thorn" with patient prayer to God and not with anger, bitterness or resentment. Three times he asked God to take away the thorn, but the Lord answered, "My grace is sufficient for you, for my power is made perfect in weakness" (12:9). In other words, "No." What was Paul's response? Not anger or resentment, but faith: "Therefore I will boast all the more gladly about my weaknesses, so that Christ's power may rest on me. That is why, for Christ's sake, I delight in weaknesses, in insults, in hardships, in persecutions, in difficulties. For when I am weak, then I am strong" (12:9–10). When you or I face a "thorn," a persistent weakness, and we cry to the Lord to take it away and he does not, we can follow Paul's example of faith and take strength that, even in our weakness, Christ's power can be shown. We do not need to be ashamed of the thorn, or indeed of hardships, for when we are weak we are strong in Christ. In weakness, then, we ask "How is Christ's strength shown in my life?"

Often we need even more specific examples to show us the way. I mentioned the man who showed me how he would "pray continually" in the office. The principle could be extended in many ways to bring prayer into the every day: maybe to pray before putting on the kettle; or to stop at set times of the day to pray.

Another practical example is the story of a business leader who devoted a certain percentage of his very first income to the Lord's work. He gave the same proportion even as his success grew so that by the time he became very wealthy he had already been very generous. He had honoured the Lord with little and also with much because he practised the same principle of giving.

When I asked my fellow-preachers for sample exemplary stories, they gave the following:

- The minister who with his wife decided each year to give away a greater percentage of their income than the year before. Sometimes that increase was very small, maybe less than 1 percent, but they stuck to that commitment to grow in generosity.
- Artists and musicians who write SDG on their works or at the end of their manuscripts. SDG stands for *soli Deo gloria*, latin for "Glory to God alone." It is a reminder that the work was produced for the sake of praising God, and not for humans' glory.
- When entering a room or a church, do we "walk toward the pain"? Sometimes there will be a person on their own because others are awkwardly avoiding them for some reason: perhaps because they have been bereaved or caught up in some tragic event. No-one knows what to say. Make it your habit to head towards the person that everyone else is avoiding. For example gently say you're sorry for what they are facing. Or just greet them. Walk towards the pain.
- A related example is of a church that was facing tensions over a particular issue. Each Sunday this family would choose to sit with some of the people on the other side of the argument. In fact on the way to church their children would ask which of three or so families they were sitting with that week.
- God had put mission to the Middle East on the heart of Mack Styles. He had gathered a team and needed only to sell their house in the US. On the day before the house was due to go on the market, the 9/11 attack took place (11th September 2001). Two of the attackers were from the very region that Mack had planned to move to. Friends tried to dissuade them from going but they persevered in following what they felt to be God's call. Because of their faithfulness and persistence, two decades of ministry to the Muslim world followed.[1]
- A practical application of Jesus's teaching that, "If your right eye causes you to stumble, gouge it out and throw it away. It is better for you to lose one part of your body than for your whole body to be thrown into hell" (Matt 5:29; see also Matt 18:8–9 and Mark 9:43–47) is to take radical action against the temptation to pornography. If the temptation comes through buying magazines, a person can change their route home from work to

---

1. See https://www.desiringgod.org/articles/give-me-nineteen-men (accessed April 2022).

avoid a certain shop; the temptation today is more likely to be in accessing pornography through the internet: the radical action there is to give up a smart phone in favour of a "dumb phone" that can only send texts and make phone calls.

- As an example of what to pray before reading the Bible, I have given the example of praying I-O-U-S. These four prayers orient my heart and mind to God that I may receive his word rightly:

I = **Incline** my heart to your testimonies, and not to selfish gain! (Psalm 119:36)

O = **Open** my eyes, that I may behold wondrous things out of your law. (Psalm 119:18)

U = **Teach** me your way, O LORD, that I may walk in your truth; **unite** my heart to fear your name. (Psalm 86:11)

S = **Satisfy** us in the morning with your steadfast love, that we may rejoice and be glad all our days. (Psalm 90:14).[2]

I acknowledge that these examples may reflect my context more than yours. They may not be suitable for your sermons and for your hearers and you will need to find examples that are closer to home. Often there will be testimony from within your own congregation that you can use as exemplary stories – if you can find the time and opportunity to ask. Once again this is where preparation in advance is helpful: if you know that your sermon will feature a particular application, you could make time in the week to talk with one or two mature believers and ask them what putting that into practice has meant for them at work or at home or in their studies.

Practical examples make it harder for hearers to duck when the sermon is aimed at them. If the sermon application is "too vague, too abstract, or too predictable, nobody will think it applies to anybody."[3] They will think, "That does not apply to me." But when we give practical examples that relate to what they face, then they will see that God's word does apply to them! We do not have to give a practical example for each group represented in the congregation. If we show what the application looks like for young and old, men and women, boys and girls, workers and students, parents and grandparents, married and single, rich and poor, local and foreigner, it would bore everyone. One good solution is to make a specific practical example for a first group and show

---

2. Summarised from the first chapter of Matt Smethurst, *Before You Open Your Bible: Nine Heart Postures for Approaching God's Word* (10Publishing, 2019).

3. Allan Chapple, *Preaching: A Guidebook for Beginners* (London: Latimer Trust, 2013), 87.

how this could be rolled out to others.[4] If an individual has been caught in a specific sin, we do not name that person in the sermon ("John Smith, this is about YOU!") but speak about the kinds of people the verse describes, and make sure to find a way to talk with John Smith individually, beforehand if at all possible. It is less embarrassing to say that so-and-so is a good example, but here too we might protect the person's name. We can say "I know a person who . . ." or perhaps "Even this week I was chatting with someone who . . ." I think this is similar to what Paul is doing when he says, "I know a man in Christ who fourteen years ago was caught up to the third heaven. Whether it was in the body or out of the body I do not know – God knows" (2 Cor 12:2). He seems to be speaking about himself but keeps that in the background so that Christ can be in the foreground.

Practical examples without biblical teaching become law. We are more likely to remember the practical teaching than the principle behind it. I have had members of the congregation plead, "Just tell us what to *do*." It is tempting for them to ask this, and tempting for me to give them what they want. And wrong in both cases. For example we mentioned above the exemplary stories of applying the command to "pray continually" by including prayer in the every day or even stopping the day to pray. It is one thing to do this as a chosen discipline, another as a compulsory regime. Other religions will pray before opening a tap, or will stop several times a day to pray: while this is effective in bringing their religion into the everyday, it does not bring *Christian discipleship* into the everyday. It is not enough to tell people what to do: we must always be clear on why we are doing it. Exemplary stories that do not link back to the biblical truth have ceased to serve the exposition of God's word: they have instead become laws that will obscure God's word of grace. Paul tells us that mere rules lack any value in restraining sensual indulgence (Col 2:23) and so we must teach the truth and *then* give practical examples.

Exercise

Look up one of your recent sermons and identify the application sections.
State the application in one sentence.

_____

_____

---

4. Chapell, *Christ-Centered Preaching*, 225.

Did you give an exemplary story? If not, write one now.

_____

_____

If you gave one exemplary story, did you give others? If not, how could one or two others be given to illustrate how the general principle could be rolled out to other situations?

_____

_____

If you found this hard (and I expect you did), what can you do differently in preparing your next sermons to provide your congregation with more practical examples of the applications your sermon demands?

_____

_____

6

Where Do I Find Stories?

Emma Woodhouse delights in finding suitable husbands for her friends. She is usually very pleased with the results (and with herself, it must be said). When it comes to her own marriage, it's a different story. No man is good enough for her, it seems. Eventually she realizes how blind she has been: she has consistently ignored Mr. Knightley, who is kind, considerate and capable. He was there all the time![1]

The most important part of looking for little stories that we can use in preaching is to open our eyes and see what is in front of us. Our daily life will turn out to be full of Mr. Knightleys (for preaching, that is, not marriage!). This means learning to be alert, creative and intentional.

Be Alert

Once we begin to see our daily life through the eyes of little stories, we can begin to notice incidents and situations. This is what Jesus himself did. "Jesus looked around and found illustrations in ordinary people and their possessions. He used the events of nature and the activities of people to make his lessons and sermons easier to learn and remember."[2]

Familiar stories and images help to connect: people we know or people who are like people we know, stories we know or that are common to our culture, things we use all the time or see others using, things we see, hear, taste, touch and smell, such as plants, food, water and animals.[3] One of the challenges for me in writing this book is that I do not know the lives of my readers and it is

---

1. The characters are taken from the novel *Emma* by Jane Austen.

2. Langham Partnership, *Helps: 40 Simple and Memorable Teaching and Preaching Resources*, vol. 1 (Carlisle: Langham Preaching Resources, 2017), 14, Help #11.

3. Langham Partnership, *Helps*, vol. 1, 3, Help #2.

difficult for me to find familiar stories. If you have noticed that challenge and it makes you determined to do better in your preaching, then I am content.

We can find little stories – that is, images, short parables, longer stories – in the everyday events that we experience. We can see the things that our congregation know, the people they know, the stories they know, and look for points of connection. We simply need to be alert: "Preachers who illustrate well do not wait passively for the world to offer them something significant to note. Rather they steal from the world the treasures others do not notice or do not have the opportunity to display."[4]

This takes practice and it takes skill. But it can be learned. Sometimes at a preaching conference, participants are asked to spend thirty minutes walking around to look for something that will act as a little story in the sermon outline that they have been working on.[5] At first they find it a hopeless task, but then their eyes begin to see: a tiny plant holding on for dear life in the crack of a paving stone becomes a short parable of fragile faith in the face of great opposition; or the stallholder carefully arranging his or her wares so that the most attractive side is facing the customer mirrors how we carefully arrange our own lives so that the most attractive side is facing the onlooker; or the way that traffic responds to the police officer's whistle and hand-signals, and what this says about the citizens' respect (or disrespect!) for the rule of law. Many little stories are already there, waiting for us to see them. They are everywhere. They are free of charge, too! We need to be alert.

Be a Learner

We can also learn from others. The first way we can do this is through listening to good preaching for ourselves, so that we can see the preacher's skill. One of my aims in writing this book is to help you see what good preachers do so that you can appreciate it and learn from it.

We can also learn to be creative. This will be especially important if your education and training have encouraged remembering and repetition over independent thought. Writing sermons and thinking of little stories that fit is just as creative as painting a picture or building a sculpture. If you think about it, we too are painting and building, but with words. Creativity and ideas need space in which to grow. Usually that means finding a time of day when our minds are not overtired or filled with other things; it may mean finding a

---

4. Chapell, *Christ-Centered Preaching*, 191.
5. See Langham Partnership, *Helps*, vol. 2, 27, Help #59.

place where we are free to think. And often it also means not working at the last minute but at a time when ideas can come more freely.

We can help one another to be creative. Maybe we can even challenge each other: "Here is an incident: how would you use it as a little story in a sermon?" Or, "Here is a truth: now tell me a story that will help me understand it." This is practice, just as kicking a football around prepares for a game, or strumming on an instrument prepares for a song.

We can also learn to be creative by taking an interest in others' lives. One way is by reading for enjoyment: let us stop from time to time to appreciate the view, to note the writer's skill, and to capture an image or little story that will serve the preaching. We can also learn by listening to others, and by asking open questions that will allow them to describe their world, their thoughts, their emotions. All of this is opening our eyes to see what has been there all along.

As you become more familiar with what makes explanatory stories, motivational stories and exemplary stories work well, you should be able to see how and why others' stories work well. It may be as you listen to others preaching but it may be as you listen to presentations outside of the church setting: why is this speaker so persuasive? Why does that poster make me desire that product? When we find that we are struck by an image, a story, an idea, we can ask, "Why does this make me feel like that?" and then "Is there any way I can turn this into a little story that can serve the preaching of the word?"

Set Your Nets

New Zealand is an island nation surrounded by excellent fishing waters. Although other nations are permitted to send their fishing fleets into New Zealand waters, they are closely monitored. My brother once worked as a fishing monitor. Trawlers do not simply collect every fish they sail over: if their nets are set just right they will catch just the target fish. My brother's role was to check that the nets being used matched the permitted catch.

If we are being alert in everyday life, ready to capture little stories from everyday life, we will be like those trawlers whose nets are set to catch the fish they sail through. And like the trawlers, we cannot collect everything or we would sink. So how do we set our nets to catch the right stories? Like the fishing fleets we need to know in advance what we are looking for. That is why it is good to begin preparing sermons in advance. Regular preachers can begin on Monday so that by Tuesday an outline is already forming. As you go through the week with your eyes open, you have an idea of what you want to illustrate. You begin to trawl with a purpose because your nets are set for a particular sermon.

I think this also helps us approach using the Internet. There are sites with sermon illustrations but they need to be used with great caution. First, the little stories they give may not be the right stories for our passage, as we explored above. Second, they may not connect with your people. Even though I live in the Western world, I find that little stories about the American Civil War do not connect with my congregation. I think the Internet can be helpful for recalling a particular news story so that I can be sure to have the correct details. I have two rules in mind when searching the Internet like this: first, I must be very clear about what I am looking for; and second, I set a time limit on my search.

Finally, let's not forget that the Bible is a good source of stories that will work as explanatory stories, as we saw in Matthew 24:36–44. See the section in chapter 2 "(C) Helpful Cross References That Can Help You to Illustrate Your Passage."

Be a Collector

Sometimes stories come to us unannounced and it is a good idea to keep a notebook or its digital equivalent. Make a note of the source so that you can look up the details if you need to use the little story. Whatever we use, let us be sure to quote stories as accurately as we can. If we invent stories of daily life, we should make that clear.

Summary and Conclusion

This book has been about using little stories to serve expository preaching. They can do so within the points of a sermon or between the points of the sermon. They can help with understanding, application or motivation. They can sharpen the focus of the whole sermon. But above all they serve the sermon rather than swallow it up. We have also suggested where to find stories and how to keep using them better. Preaching is an art that takes time. The first fifty years are the hardest, apparently!

It has been my hope to leave you better equipped for the wonderful task of communicating God's truth. The true benefit will come when you put this into practice and make it fit your personality and gifts.

And why does it matter? Here is what Augustine of Hippo wrote about working at skill in speaking:

> Since rhetoric is used to give conviction to both truth and falsehood, who could dare to maintain that truth, which depends on us for its defence, should stand unarmed in the fight against falsehood? This would mean that those who are trying to give conviction to their falsehoods would . . . expound falsehoods in descriptions that are succinct, lucid and convincing, while we would expound the truth in such a way as to bore our listeners, cloud their understanding and stifle their desire to believe; that they would assail the truth and advocate falsehood with fallacious arguments, while we would be too feeble either to defend what is true or refute what is false.[1]

---

1. Augustine, *On Christian Teaching*, 101.

Appendix

The Five Foundational Values of Expository Preaching

Explanatory, motivational and exemplary stories serve a particular kind of preaching. Expository preaching aims to open up what a Bible passage says so that the message can be applied to the hearers. Other kinds of preaching will take a theme and find a text to hang it on, but expository preaching invites the text to set the theme of the sermon. As noted in the introduction, Timothy Keller lists the other kinds of preaching as evangelistic (to convey truth to non-believers), doctrinal or catechetical (to instruct believers), festal (to celebrate events in the church year such as Easter and Christmas) and prophetic (to speak to a particular historical or cultural moment).[1]

Expository preaching is built on a foundation of values and it is these rather than the practice of using stories or making points which make preaching expository. We might say that just as the French Republic hopes that the values of "Liberté, égalité, fraternité" (freedom, equality, brotherhood) lie at the heart of its national life, so preachers should have the five values of conviction, faithfulness, relevance, clarity and integrity at the heart of their expository ministry.[2]

Conviction is the belief that the Bible is God's written, inspired and authoritative word. If we believe this we will speak God's words rather than our own, just as a herald will proclaim the king's words and not his own. If we do not believe that the Bible's message is true then we will be tempted to whisper it in a corner or, worse, mingle our own thoughts with God's holy words. The conviction that God has spoken and that his message is in the Bible underlies

---

1. Keller, *Preaching*, 30, following Hughes Oliphant Old.

2. I am grateful to those who both modelled and taught these values to me. I owe the terms used here (conviction, faithfulness, relevance, clarity and integrity) to Langham Preaching, an organization devoted to helping the growth of national expository preaching movements across the world.

the whole enterprise of expository preaching. We let the text speak because God speaks through his inspired word.

Faithfulness to the text means that we must pass on everything that we receive from God through this passage of Scripture. In that sense we are stewards entrusted with a message which we are to pass on faithfully – without adding or removing parts along the way. That is why we must work to understand each passage in its context, within the chapter, within the book and within the whole Bible. When we start a sermon in a text, we stay in that text. We do not preach "Safari sermons" that journey from one text to another.[3] Faithful preaching starts in the passage, stays in the passage and usually ends in the passage.[4]

Relevance recognizes that God's word speaks to us today because it is a living word (Heb 4:12). Relevance flows from faithfulness because when we apply what the passage teaches, we are applying what God teaches. We have to work to ensure that we are making *Christian* applications when preaching from Old Testament passages. We also work to ensure that the applications are practical. But chiefly we must be bold in making the applications that flow from the teaching of the passage. This is especially important when the applications are uncomfortable! Paul knew this when he asked the Christians at Ephesus to pray that he would preach with courage: "Pray also for me, that whenever I speak, words may be given me so that I will fearlessly make known the mystery of the gospel, for which I am an ambassador in chains. Pray that I may declare it fearlessly, as I should" (Eph 6:19–20).

Clarity. A clear sermon is like clean glass that shows our hard work in being faithful and relevant. An unclear sermon is like a window with the blind closed. Paul paid careful attention to his communication even though he claimed not to be a polished speaker. He did not dazzle his hearers with fancy speaking tricks but he used his skill to make the truth plain and clear, as he explains: "When I came to you, I did not come with eloquence or human wisdom as I proclaimed to you the testimony about God. For I resolved to know nothing while I was with you except Jesus Christ and him crucified" (1 Cor 2:1–2). He even asked the Christians in Colossae to pray for him that he might be clear in proclaiming the message: "And pray for us, too, that God may open a door for our message, so that we may proclaim the mystery of Christ, for which I am in chains. Pray that I may proclaim it clearly, as I should" (Col 4:3–4).

---

3. "Safari" is an East African word meaning "journey."

4. See the section in chapter 2 on cross references for exceptions: "Using Biblical Stories and Cross-References Properly."

Clarity means effective communication. It requires a deep understanding of what we are trying to say and a determination to do everything in our power to bring it within the reach of our hearers. Only when we understand an idea deeply can we express it simply. Try asking a person to describe his or her work to you in one sentence and you will quickly find out whether that person knows what he or she is doing! Explanatory stories are vital to achieving clarity.

Integrity. The final value relates to the character of the preacher. Integrity means that our mouths and our lives give the same message. Jesus had strong words for those who do not practise what they preach:

> The teachers of the law and the Pharisees sit in Moses' seat. So you must be careful to do everything they tell you. But do not do what they do, for they do not practise what they preach. They tie up heavy, cumbersome loads and put them on other people's shoulders, but they themselves are not willing to lift a finger to move them. (Matt 23:2–4)

False teachers are people who claim to know God but deny him by their actions. Paul says that they are "detestable, disobedient and unfit for doing anything good" (Titus 1:16). Hypocrisy of this kind can spread: "Many will follow their depraved conduct and will bring the way of truth into disrepute. In their greed these teachers will exploit you with fabricated stories. Their condemnation has long been hanging over them, and their destruction has not been sleeping" (2 Pet 2:2–3).

It is because of these false teachers that faithful teachers must show that integrity of message and life. The faithful elder's character and message must be aligned: "He must hold firmly to the trustworthy message as it has been taught, so that he can encourage others by sound doctrine and refute those who oppose it" (Titus 1:9). We know how easy it is for a moment's sin to undo an hour's preaching – however faithfully prepared.

Conviction, faithfulness, relevance, clarity and integrity are the foundation on which expository preaching is built. Explanatory, motivational and exemplary stories used in the service of these values can be of real help in preaching. And then they become stories that truly serve.

Acknowledgements

I want to thank all those whose preaching and teaching modelled the principles to me so that I in turn can share them with others. My thanks to those who have attended preaching seminars with me: your questions have sharpened my understanding.

I also want to thank Langham Preaching's Global Leadership Team who took time to work through the book and gave very helpful feedback. A special mention goes to Paul Windsor and Jennifer Cuthbertson for help with the section on where to find stories and how to be creative, and to Paul Windsor and Mark Meynell for their enthusiastic support of this project.

Langham Literature and its imprints are a ministry of Langham Partnership.

Langham Partnership is a global fellowship working in pursuit of the vision God entrusted to its founder John Stott –

to facilitate the growth of the church in maturity and Christ-likeness through raising the standards of biblical preaching and teaching.

Our vision is to see churches in the Majority World equipped for mission and growing to maturity in Christ through the ministry of pastors and leaders who believe, teach and live by the word of God.

Our mission is to strengthen the ministry of the word of God through:
- nurturing national movements for biblical preaching
- fostering the creation and distribution of evangelical literature
- enhancing evangelical theological education

especially in countries where churches are under-resourced.

Our ministry

Langham Preaching partners with national leaders to nurture indigenous biblical preaching movements for pastors and lay preachers all around the world. With the support of a team of trainers from many countries, a multi-level programme of seminars provides practical training, and is followed by a programme for training local facilitators. Local preachers' groups and national and regional networks ensure continuity and ongoing development, seeking to build vigorous movements committed to Bible exposition.

Langham Literature provides Majority World preachers, scholars and seminary libraries with evangelical books and electronic resources through publishing and distribution, grants and discounts. The programme also fosters the creation of indigenous evangelical books in many languages, through writer's grants, strengthening local evangelical publishing houses, and investment in major regional literature projects, such as one volume Bible commentaries like *The Africa Bible Commentary* and *The South Asia Bible Commentary*.

Langham Scholars provides financial support for evangelical doctoral students from the Majority World so that, when they return home, they may train pastors and other Christian leaders with sound, biblical and theological teaching. This programme equips those who equip others. Langham Scholars also works in partnership with Majority World seminaries in strengthening evangelical theological education. A growing number of Langham Scholars study in high quality doctoral programmes in the Majority World itself. As well as teaching the next generation of pastors, graduated Langham Scholars exercise significant influence through their writing and leadership.

To learn more about Langham Partnership and the work we do visit **langham.org**

Ingram Content Group UK Ltd.
Milton Keynes UK
UKHW020011060523
421276UK00009B/156